Scattered

SCATTERED

The Forced Relocation of Poland's Ukrainians after World War II

Diana Howansky Reilly

The University of Wisconsin Press

Publication of this volume has been made possible, in part,
through support from
the **Andrew W. Mellon Foundation.**

The University of Wisconsin Press
1930 Monroe Street, 3rd Floor
Madison, Wisconsin 53711-2059
uwpress.wisc.edu

3 Henrietta Street
London WC2E 8LU, England
eurospanbookstore.com

Printed in the United States of America

Library of Congress Cataloging-in-Publication Data

Reilly, Diana Howansky.
Scattered: the forced relocation of Poland's Ukrainians
after World War II / Diana Howansky Reilly.
p.   cm.
Includes bibliographical references and index.
ISBN 978-0-299-29340-6 (cloth: alk. paper)
ISBN 978-0-299-29343-7 (e-book)
1. Ukrainians—Poland—History—20th century.
2. Lemky—Poland—History—20th century.
3. Lemky—Poland—Biography.
4. Forced migration—Poland.
5. World War, 1939–1945—Lemkivshchyna (Poland and Slovakia)
6. Poland—History—1945–1980.
7. Lemkivshchyna (Poland and Slovakia)—History.
I. Title.
DK4438.R45   2013
940.53´14508991791—dc23
2012037002

To
my parents
who taught me about my roots

and to
my children
so they may also know about their heritage

Contents

Introduction

Although I begin the story of *Scattered*'s main characters, the Pyrtej family, at the moment when the Nazis invaded Poland in 1939, the Pyrtejs' experience with forced relocation was primarily the result of a different conflict: the long-standing discord between Poles and Ukrainians in the region. Following World War I and the dissolution of the Austro-Hungarian Empire, Poles and Ukrainians fought each other in a war over Eastern Galicia—a region on the Polish-Ukrainian border that the Allied victors eventually granted to Poland in 1923—and hostile feelings remained between the two nations. Ukrainians in Poland who were not willing to accept the status of a national minority continued to struggle for the right of self-rule. They felt that the Polish government was taking steps to assimilate them by, for example, banning the use of the Ukrainian language in government agencies and introducing reforms that turned Ukrainian-language schools into bilingual schools. Ukrainian nationalist groups began to emerge, for example the Organization of Ukrainian Nationalists (OUN), which was formed in early 1929 with the goal of overthrowing foreign rule on Ukrainian ethnographic territories and creating an independent Ukrainian state. Antagonism between Ukrainians and Poles only increased throughout the 1930s as the Polish government responded to Ukrainian resistance with aggressive tactics such as pacification campaigns. Younger members within the OUN, such as the controversial political figure Stepan Bandera, believed in the need for revolutionary action and carried out assassinations of Polish officials. The Polish government, in turn, imprisoned hundreds of Ukrainian nationalists in the Bereza Kartuska concentration camp from 1934 until the start of World War II.

Because of the growing feeling that minority groups caused conflict, the notion of creating homogeneous nation-states was also gaining popularity at this time. The work of other authors has shown that the forced migration of minority groups before the 1940s—such as the deportation of Armenians by the Ottoman Turks in 1915–17 and the transfer of the Greek population from Anatolia and the Turkish population from Greece in 1923—set a precedent and led to this becoming a common political tactic in Central and Eastern Europe during World War II and the postwar period. Both Nazi Germany and the Soviet Union, carving up Poland after 1939, wished to create a new order: Adolf Hitler deported "inferior" races and nations such as the Jews and then the Slavs from the annexed territories he wished to "Germanize," while Joseph Stalin deported national groups, including Poles as well as Ukrainians, Belorussians, and Lithuanians, he feared were collaborating with the Germans or betraying Soviet authority. When Germany then lost the war, immediately the Polish authorities expelled the German population from Western Pomerania, and the Czechoslovak authorities expelled the Sudeten Germans from Czech lands. Meanwhile, the international community, including Britain and the United States—which had also implemented the concept of collective responsibility during the war by rounding up Americans of Japanese heritage and placing them in internment camps— accepted forced migration as a means of preventing further conflict between ethnicities and promoting peace. The Pyrtej family's story progresses against this backdrop: first they face the Soviet-Polish population exchange from 1944 to 1946 and then they experience the forced relocation of the Ukrainian minority in Poland in 1947 known as Akcja Wisła (Operation Vistula).

The Pyrtejs found themselves on the Ukrainian side of the Polish-Ukrainian conflict, but the identity of the family and their people is more complex. For generations, the Pyrtejs had lived in the Lemko region (Lemkivshchyna in Ukrainian; Łemkowszczyzna in Polish), located in current-day southeastern Poland. Debate surrounds the self-identification and settlement of the people of this region. The Lemkos, a compact group of highlanders who inhabited the outer Carpathian Mountains, practiced Eastern rite Christianity, spoke an East Slavic vernacular, used the Cyrillic alphabet, and made their living through farming and forestry before they were removed from their homeland in the 1940s. Lemkos formerly referred to themselves as Rusyns (Ruthenians, in English), a name harking back to the kingdom of Kievan Rus', which had stretched to the Carpathians during the Middle Ages. However, in the period leading up to World War II, because of the various national and religious movements battling to claim them, the people of the Lemko region divided into three different orientations: those who identified with the Ukrainian national movement; those who supported Moscophilism, seeing themselves as part of a Russian people; and those who supported Rusophilism, seeing themselves as part of a common East Slavic people. There is also no agreement regarding the origins of the Lemkos. Ukrainian scholars have stated that the ancestors of the Lemkos were members of a tribe called the White Croats, who first migrated through the Carpathians as early as the fifth and sixth centuries, remained there, became part of Kievan Rus', and organized new settlements in the Lemko region. Polish scholars, on the other hand, have stated that the Lemko region remained essentially uninhabited until the fourteenth century, when it was separated into landowners' estates and, to make these estates profitable, noblemen encouraged the settlement of villages by migrating shepherds known as the Vlachs, who eventually mixed with Rusyn farmers also moving to these territories.

Within the Lemko region itself, further distinctions should be made between the eastern and western halves, divided roughly at the Dukla Pass in the Carpathian Mountains. The Pyrtej family lived in the village of Smerekowiec, located in the western half of the Lemko region, where Moscophilism and Rusophilism tended to be more widespread. The eastern half of the Lemko region, on the other hand, was more influenced in the early twentieth century by the Ukrainian national movement emerging from Eastern Galicia and generally suffered more violence during military operations carrying out resettlement to Soviet Ukraine. In the first months of 1946, for example, the Polish army brutally resettled Lemkos from the Sanok and Lesko Districts in the eastern Lemko region. Numerous cases of Polish soldiers killing Lemko civilians, including priests, women, and children, were documented.

This book does not wade far into the debate over Lemko identity, though, because Poland's postwar government ultimately included anyone considering himself or herself a Lemko or a Rusyn within the Ukrainian population to be relocated. For instance, inhabitants of the village of Komańcza in the eastern Lemko region sent petitions to Polish officials, asking to be exempted from resettlement to Soviet Ukraine because they did not feel themselves to be Ukrainian. For clarification of the Lemkos' origins, officials contacted a professor at the Polish Academy of Sciences, who responded that it was difficult to provide an answer about the essence of the Lemkos. He explained that the Lemkos regarded themselves as Rusyns, spoke a dialect that was distinct from literary Ukrainian, and were "less chauvinist" than nationalist Ukrainians. A few days later, ignoring the professor's answer, the officials issued orders that the Lemkos should be evacuated.

Historical evidence has shown that the Polish government's motive for forcibly relocating the Ukrainian population in Poland in the 1940s, which culminated in Operation Vistula, was not just to liquidate the Ukrainian nationalists (the OUN as well as its military wing, the Ukrainian Insurgent Army [UPA]) but to get rid of the entire Ukrainian minority, which the government viewed as a long-standing problem. The government "solved" this problem by deporting, dispersing, and pressuring that minority (including the Lemkos) to assimilate into the Polish population. This was ethnic cleansing, defined as "the attempt to create ethnically homogeneous geographic areas through the deportation or forcible displacement of persons belonging to particular ethnic groups." The Pyrtej family, who had not supported the politics of the Ukrainian nationalists, were relocated because of their ethnicity. As a consequence of the policies of the Polish postwar government, the Ukrainian minority lost its ancestral territories, and Poland's cultural diversity deteriorated. The regional culture of the Lemkos has also been threatened with extinction. Without a compact community like the one that existed for centuries in the Lemko region, the unique customs and vernacular of the Lemkos— whether defined as a Ukrainian dialect or as a separate language—are in danger of disappearing.

What *Scattered* seeks to contribute to the understanding of the Soviet-Polish population exchange and Operation Vistula is an authentic bottom-up perspective of this history. Written largely in the journalistic tradition of "show, don't tell," the book gives a voice (as much as possible in the unique Lemko vernacular) to individuals in the western Lemko region who lived through this history—to ordinary people who lived through extraordinary events. *Scattered* is a work of nonfiction, and

Introduction

I have not made up any of the details I have described. As explained further in the prologue, the main characters in the book are members of my family, which allowed me greater access to them. All the events are reconstructed based on a multitude of taped interviews with individuals who had personal knowledge of those events, checked where possible against facts from primary and secondary source materials. The descriptions are, therefore, reconstructions of memories and interpretations of events. The dialogue that appears within quotation marks is direct quotation (or translation of quotation) from the individuals interviewed as they remembered conversations. Commenting on the challenge and ethics of writing narrative nonfiction, the editor Jack Hart stated:

> Any reconstructed narrative, even an account by a reliable eyewitness, is an approximation of what really happened, and some postmodernist types interpret that to mean no external reality exists. For purely practical reasons, I can't buy that argument. The most important purpose of nonfiction narrative is to help us cope with a challenging world. The closer we come to portraying that world accurately, the more helpful our stories will be. No, we'll never get it absolutely right, and we'll never find an absolute consensus on much of anything. But the only ethical approach is to get as close as possible.

In 1946 another journalist and author, George Orwell, criticized the use of empty language as he wrote about the forced migration of that time in his essay "Politics and the English Language":

> Millions of peasants are robbed of their farms and sent trudging along the roads with no more than they can carry: this is called *transfer of population* or *rectification of frontiers*. People are imprisoned for years without trial, or shot in the back of the neck or sent to die of scurvy in Arctic lumber camps: this is called *elimination of unreliable elements*. Such phraseology is needed if one wants to name things without calling up mental pictures of them. . . . The inflated style itself is a kind of euphemism. A mass of Latin words falls upon the facts like soft snow, blurring the outline and covering up all the details.

By relating the true stories of the Pyrtej family and the people with whom they came into contact, *Scattered* attempts to get as close as possible to the reality they experienced. Those who survived these events have spoken in the vivid language of personal memory, their words sweeping away the euphemisms to provide a sharp, detailed mental picture of the forced relocation of Poland's Ukrainians after World War II.

Note on Transliteration and Translation

I have used the Library of Congress system for transliterating Cyrillic into English for all Ukrainian, Lemko, and Russian words and phrases. I verified spellings of words in Lemko with the help of Petro Pyrtej's own work, *Korotkyi slovnyk lemkivs'kykh hovirok* (Ivano-Frankivsk: Siversiia MB, 2004). Throughout *Scattered*, I have chosen to use the Polish spelling of villages in the Lemko region rather than the Lemko spelling (e.g., Smerekowiec vs. Smerekovets; Piorunka vs. Perunka), so that readers can easily find these locations on current-day maps. I have also included the original-language version of a quotation rather than just the English translation when I felt that readers would benefit from it, such as to get a feeling for the pronunciation and flavor of the Lemko vernacular or to understand the exact wording of the Polish government's orders to assimilate the Ukrainian minority. All transliterations and translations are my own, unless noted otherwise.

Scattered

Prologue

The Realization

W hat do you mean, the Polish government kicked you out of your home?" I asked my mother when I was a teenager. I cannot recall exactly how old I was or how this conversation with my mother even started. But I remember standing in the kitchen of our comfortable suburban house in upscale Wilton, Connecticut, trying to absorb the discovery that the Polish government had forced my entire family, along with tens of thousands of other people, out of southern Poland in 1947 through a secret plan code-named Akcja Wisła, or Operation Vistula.

My parents never kept this information from me. Since childhood, I had known that both of my parents, both sets of my grandparents, and many generations of my ancestors before them were born in the territory called Lemkivshchyna, the Lemko region, in the outer Carpathian Mountains of what is now southeastern Poland. I had been well aware that our people, the Lemkos, were not Poles by nationality but members of an ethnic group whom many, such as my parents, considered to be Ukrainians, while many others referred to them as Rusyns. I had grown up immersed in the Ukrainian American community, attending Ukrainian school every Saturday, Ukrainian folk-dancing practice every Tuesday, and sleep-away camp for Ukrainian youth every summer. In Ukrainian school I had learned that, since at least the mid-nineteenth century, the Lemkos were thought to have received this name because they always used the word *lem*, meaning "only." Yet, until this conversation in the kitchen, I had somehow never either paid attention to or fully understood the details of my family's removal from their native land against their will.

For the first time, I listened as my mother described how she was a baby when Polish soldiers came to her village—as they did to my father's village and hundreds of other villages throughout the region—and ordered everyone to pack whatever few belongings they could fit into their horse-drawn wagons. The Polish army evacuated the villagers that same day, including scores of my great-aunts, great-uncles, and other relatives by both blood and marriage, and soon shipped them by train in cattle cars across the country to western Poland. Not until more than a decade after Operation Vistula did each set of my grandparents finally manage to emigrate with their children from western Poland to the United States, where my parents—Stefan Howansky and Mary Nadia Lozyniak—met at a Lemko wedding in Connecticut, married a few years later, and had my brother, my sister, and me.

In the summer of 1992, just after my freshman year away at college, my parents took my siblings and me to see the Lemko region for the first time. We flew into Berlin, where it was easier to rent a car, since newly democratic Poland was still at the beginning of its transition to a free-market economy. In a big, blue, borrowed Volkswagen minivan, we set out in the direction of the Polish border, riding by remnants of the Berlin Wall and stopping to collect a few chipped-off pieces of the graffiti-painted concrete to bring back home. We crossed into Poland and headed southeast, finding overnight accommodations when and where necessary. We drove for hours, until the terrain transformed into the low, rolling mountains of the Lower Beskyd range of the Carpathians, once the home of the Lemkos.

Passing yellow and green strips of farmland and grazing cows, we entered the village of Żdynia, not only where my father was born but where we knew the annual Łemkowska Watra festival was taking place. Every summer since 1982, members of an organization called the Union of Lemkos coordinated this three-day festival in the Lemko region to remember and celebrate their people's roots. The name Łemkowska Watra means "Lemko Bonfire," one of which was always lit at the start of the event, symbolizing the desire among Lemkos for their culture to blaze eternally, despite their expulsion. I watched as thousands of Lemkos now living throughout Poland, Ukraine, Slovakia, the United States, and Canada returned to their ancestral land to spend time together. Car after

Modern Poland

car turned off the one main road in sleepy Żdynia and onto a pathway in the middle of a wild grass field to reach the festival site, surrounded by tree-covered hills. People pitched their multicolored tents all across these hills, trying to get the best view possible of the large festival stage below. The stage, built in a shape reminiscent of a traditional wooden Lemko house with a sloping, triangular rooftop, featured nonstop performances of Lemko song and dance.

The festival organizers invited my father, a local leader in Lemko affairs in the United States, to say a few words in Ukrainian onstage. I listened as he spoke about being five years old during the summer of 1947 but still remembering how Polish soldiers came to his house to arrest his father, Damian Howansky, for allegedly supporting the Ukrainian nationalist groups that were active in the region. The soldiers tried to calm down Damian's sobbing wife by saying that they were just taking her husband for questioning, but they actually imprisoned him in a concentration camp in the city of Jaworzno for seven months. My father then spoke about how his family prepared for Operation Vistula. He packed a pair of children's skis that a village boy had given him; he had been excited to try them out that winter. Not understanding that his family did not have room to take everything, he started to cry when his grandfather, Emilian Howansky, threw the skis off the top of the already overloaded wagon and refused to take them. My father also spoke about how his family's land in Żdynia once extended to a portion of the festival site, including the exact stage area where he was now standing. After the Polish government relocated them, however, his parents never had the chance to see the Lemko region again, having passed away in the United States.

As the Łemkowska Watra came to a close, we climbed back into our minivan and drove not more than ten minutes north to Smerekowiec, the village where my mother had lived before Operation Vistula. My mother could not show us much, though, because the village life that she had known no longer existed. Her family's one-room, thatched-roof, wooden house had burned down, and she knew practically nobody in the village, since only a few Lemkos had eventually returned. Still, we visited the village's Greek Catholic church, where my mother had been christened and her parents had been married. The church was constructed in the traditional Lemko style, with three onion domes of different heights. We also visited the village cemetery, where the grave of my mother's great-grandmother stood amid overgrown wildflowers. The grave's headstone was hand-carved in the shape of a large Greek Catholic cross with three bars bearing the crucified body of Jesus Christ. My mother's great-grandmother, who died in 1920, was among the last members of my family to be buried in Smerekowiec.

Riding up and over a small mountain known as Magura, we departed the Lemko region and traveled back across the country. We stopped in the western Polish town of Kożuchów, where my maternal grandmother's younger sister—whose name was Anna but whom everyone called Hania—still lived. A rare all-family gathering had been planned at Hania's house, with my maternal grandparents flying in from the United States and my grandmother's older brother, Petro, journeying from Ukraine as well.

By the time we all descended upon the house in Kożuchów, my grandmother, my great-aunt Hania, and my great-uncle Petro were sitting in lawn chairs in the backyard, talking with one another as if they had never been separated. Although the three siblings had grown up together in Smerekowiec, Petro had resettled in Soviet Ukraine just before Operation Vistula, my grandmother had immigrated to the United States in the early 1960s, and Hania had stayed behind in western Poland. Petro was the scholar among the three, having finished university, completed graduate school courses, and worked as a Ukrainian- and German-language teacher in the western Ukrainian city of Ivano-Frankivsk, known previously as Stanisławów. My grandmother Melania did not have the opportunity to study beyond grammar school, ending up as a cleaning lady in the United States, sending dollars back to her family in Poland and Ukraine whenever she could; but she still never hesitated to challenge the opinions of her brother. Hania, sixteen and thirteen years younger than her brother and sister, respectively, always just seemed to show a sweet deference to the both of them.

Petro and Hania had each visited the United States, but never before had I seen my grandmother with both of them at once. Only years later, when Petro passed away in 1999, did I realize that my first trip to see my ancestors' homeland was the last time that my grandmother, her brother, and her sister were all together again.

I returned to the United States, to my American life—finishing college, landing a job, going back to graduate school. Underlying everything, though, was a desire to learn more about the resettlement of my family and hundreds of thousands of members of the Ukrainian minority in Poland. I studied history and international affairs, taking classes about Eastern Europe and the World War II period. Personal recollections of Operation Vistula were rarely mentioned in the English-language history books, however, so I made my way back to Poland on a Fulbright grant with the idea of finding and interviewing remaining victims of the 1947 relocation plan. For what turned out to be two years, from 1998 to 2000, I traveled around both the Lemko region and western Poland with a backpack on my shoulders and a tape recorder at the ready, speaking with dozens of people who were willing to tell me their stories.

Realizing that those who could remember Operation Vistula were dying one by one, I felt compelled to document the experiences of my remaining grandparents and relatives. For hours upon hours, for months if not years, I sat down with my grandmother Melania in Connecticut and collected every detail that she could recall about the periods before and after the Polish government forced her to leave the Lemko region. I spoke with family members who had immigrated to the United States after undergoing resettlement and imprisonment in the same concentration camp in Jaworzno as my paternal grandfather. I made more trips to Eastern Europe—to Poland to interview my great-aunt Hania and to explore Jaworzno, to Ukraine to interview my great-uncle Petro's wife, Olya, and to retrace the path that they took after World War II. I cross-referenced my interviews against secondary sources in Ukrainian, Polish, and English and against archival materials from the Polish secret service and the Ukrainian Insurgent Army.

All my relatives offered details of how the Polish government had removed them from their homeland, how their Lemko community had been destroyed, and how they had managed to survive in their places of resettlement. In the end, what emerged from these details was a story about a brother and two sisters from the western Lemko region—Petro, Melania, and Hania Pyrtej—who, along with their parents, spouses, in-laws, and friends, were torn apart because of politics over which they had no control. This story is a personal narrative, but at the same time it represents the experiences of many families from southeastern Poland who were considered to be part of the Ukrainian minority. What appears on the following pages is the sewing together of this narrative to create a patchwork of memories that are fading fast in the minds of those who shared them and that would have otherwise faded away forever.

1

Caught on the Battlefield of World War II

The German military convoy began to roll through the Lemko region in southern Poland during the first days of September 1939. Melania Pyrtej was watching over her family's cows as they grazed in a nearby pasture when the brown-haired seventeen-year-old saw Nazis riding by her village. The village, Smerekowiec, was named after the fir trees—*smereky*, as Lemkos like Melania called them in their native tongue—that covered the surrounding mountains. Usually, Melania led the cows farther away from home to graze all day long in the fields beneath the Magura mountain peak while she and her friends sat around talking or singing or baking potatoes over a campfire. That morning, however, her parents had warned her not to roam too far, because they were worried about what the Germans might do.

Melania watched army truck, after army truck, after army truck appear from the distance on the road stretching from the Slovakian border, only about ten kilometers away. Rumor had it that the German soldiers were resting near Lemko villages by the border and then driving up the zigzagging switchbacks over Magura toward the city of Gorlice and beyond. Melania could see soldiers' faces peering out from the backs of the green, tarp-covered vehicles as they passed by endlessly. Every few minutes or so, she thought she spotted a gap in the convoy large enough for someone to be able to cross the road, but more trucks would always appear.

The German soldiers were all riding in one direction, into Poland, since Adolf Hitler had already conquered Czechoslovakia. Less than a year earlier, on September 30, 1938, the British, French, and Italian leaders had signed the Munich Agreement in the hope that allowing Hitler to annex Czechoslovakia's German-populated Sudetenland might prevent war. Czechoslovakian planes had dropped so many leaflets into southern Poland, printed with pleas for help from the Czechs' Slavic "brothers," that the fields were strewn with sheets of paper, and Melania ran around picking them up to stop her cows from chewing and swallowing them. But the Polish government, taking advantage of Czechoslovakia's situation, instead demanded Zaolzie, its "lands beyond the Olza River," and seized this territory in October 1938 without a fight. Hitler proceeded to invade the rest of Czechoslovakia on March 15, 1939, dividing it into the German Protectorate of Bohemia and Moravia as well as a Slovak state that was a puppet of the Third Reich.

Talk had then turned to how Hitler wanted to make Poland cede the "Polish Corridor," a strip of Polish territory on the Baltic Sea that would allow him to connect the German mainland to its province of East Prussia as well as the Free City of Danzig. The Polish government, however, refused to give in to the führer's demands. So on the morning of September 1, 1939, just a few days earlier, Melania's mother, Maria, paused from her farmwork and straightened up her portly frame to watch as no fewer than seven planes soared over Smerekowiec. They were German military aircraft, the Pyrtej family learned through the village grapevine. The planes flew on to bomb a military airport, factories, and a railroad station in the town of Krosno, where Melania's twenty-year-old brother, Petro, had just that spring finished studying at a secondary school that trained teachers. The German army was invading Poland from the south, west, and north, swallowing up not just Zaolzie and the Polish Corridor but the entire western half of the country.

The local population had panicked as German motorized troops captured the town of Nowy Sącz, followed by Gorlice, in less than a week. Nobody knew whether their town would also be attacked. In some Lemko villages, closer to the lines of invasion, people loaded up as many of their belongings as possible into their wagons and hid in the woods. Finally, the people of the Lemko region realized that the German army was quickly advancing across the country and they could return safely to their homes. The well-stocked bunker that the Pyrtej family had made out of their cellar would not be needed after all.

The Polish army had underestimated Hitler's military force, and its Western allies had not sent any of the help they had promised earlier.

Now the Polish soldiers in the region, like the army brigades responsible for guarding the border, were in full retreat while the convoy of German military vehicles rolled on. Watching this German procession from the pasture, Melania could not help but feel relieved that the Poles were withdrawing, because who knew how many bombs and bullets would have flown through Smerekowiec had there been more resistance.

One morning soon after the invasion, Melania's father, Seman, short and mustached, went out to his fields to plant crops. He owned more than eighteen hectares of land—about twelve and a half of fields and six of forests, a lot by their village's standards—but the responsibility of working in the fields usually fell to Melania and her mother. Petro, the oldest son, had been away from home during the school year, while Melania's and Petro's four-year-old sister, Hania, was still much too young to help. It would be years before Hania was able to feed the chickens and geese and then graduate to tending the cows and, finally, to sowing the fields.

Seman was also gone from home often, *na furmantsi*, or hauling logs of chopped wood in his horse-drawn wagon to sell to neighboring sawmills. To help him, he would bring along Wasyl Złatykanycz, a skinny, middle-aged farmhand with a slight mental disability who had wandered from house to house looking for work until Seman took him into the Pyrtej home permanently right after Melania was born. Melania felt that her father's weeklong trips to the sawmills were a waste of time, since the cost of feeding his horses ate up most of his profit, and that it would be better if he just stayed home to take care of the pigs and other animals. However, Seman had hauled wood ever since he was young and would always complain that he needed to go whenever he felt cooped up in the family's one-room house for too long. Since the invasion, though, the Jewish owners of the old sawmill that sat on Magura had fled, and the Germans had taken control of it. So Seman decided instead to prepare the fields for the winter rye the family needed to sow. People usually planted winter rye at the end of September, not at the beginning, but Seman thought it best not to wait—he wanted to make sure the family would have enough food in the coming year.

The Pyrtej family's fields stretched far beyond their house in a long strip like a ribbon that extended up and down about three hills until they reached a forest. The fields had recently been plowed while they were wet, so the sun had dried the tilled earth into uneven lumps. Seman had started pounding the lumps with a heavy mallet in order to flatten the soil so that the winter rye could be planted and grow straight when he noticed someone watching from the bordering forest. Calmly, he put down his mallet and, so as not to scare the person off, circled around into the woods to find out who it was. He returned with a man in his early thirties who said that his name was Stanisław Barszcz. The man explained that he had been in the Polish army but fled down from Magura after the Germans attacked and his unit fled. He wanted to return to his wife in Kobylanka, a Polish village on the other side of Gorlice, but was terrified that the Germans might capture or shoot him. He was hungry and could not find anything to eat in the woods but would work for food. Seman handed him a mallet and told him to start pounding the soil.

In the afternoon, Maria carried lunch to the fields for her husband. She saw the Polish soldier, dressed in a strange mix of military boots and civilian clothing that he seemed to have exchanged for his uniform somewhere. Maria softly asked Seman whether they now had a refugee on their hands. Seman nodded and invited Stanisław to eat.

The men continued working in the field until nightfall, when Seman asked Stanisław, still shaken, back to the Pyrtej house until the immediate danger passed. Stanisław hid, covered, in the back of Seman's wagon as they rode home. He then agreed to climb up into the hay-filled loft beneath the house's thatched roof for the night rather than to sleep with everyone else in the main room of the house, where anybody passing by the window might see him. As always, Seman and Maria slept in a bed with Hania by the large brick oven that they used both to cook and to heat the house, Wasyl slept in a cozy, warm spot on top of the oven, and Melania slept on the bed that she shared with Petro.

Stanisław was still hiding in the loft the next day when the Pyrtej family resumed their farmwork. Melania milked the cows in the barn, which was connected to the house, and then took them out to pasture. She had been outside for a few hours when a gunshot in the adjacent woods suddenly made her jolt upright. One of her neighbors also working outside remarked that something had to be wrong because the Germans were firing, so Melania quickly shooed the cows home.

News swiftly passed from one house to another that the Germans had shot three men from Smerekowiec. In their haste to retreat from Magura, Polish soldiers had abandoned materials like barbed wire and lumber for barricading areas that they intended to use to defend their position. The three men from Smerekowiec, probably thinking they could use the materials to fence off their pastures or fix parts of their homes, were trying to collect them when German soldiers on patrol fired a round of bullets into the forest. One of the local men was killed, while the second was struck in the face and the third was struck in the foot. That evening, the Pyrtej family agreed that, for a while, just to be safe, they would avoid working in the section of their fields that bordered the forest; unfortunately, they had already planted some potatoes in that section.

Stanisław remained hidden for another night, and Melania got nervous when people after church the next day broke into a discussion about the new prohibition against the sheltering of any soldiers. Melania imagined the Nazis charging into their house and conducting a search. Discussions of how to help Stanisław get home ensued, with Petro climbing up into the loft several times to talk about possible plans. Finally, the Pyrtej family made arrangements with a neighbor's elderly parents, who, with no access to a phone, had traveled about ten kilometers from the village of Przysłup to Smerekowiec to make sure that their adult daughter had not been hurt during the German invasion. The parents would accompany Stanisław on the forest path back to their village, where his wife had some family.

The following morning, Stanisław Barszcz said good-bye to the Pyrtej family, although not for the last time, and stepped hesitantly out of their house, leaving with the older couple.

Day and night, the German military vehicles drove past Smerekowiec, and Melania could hear the constant, low-pitched rumbling of their engines. One day, a couple of army trucks turned in the direction of Smerekowiec onto the main road that ran through the long village. The trucks stopped close to Melania's home, and some uniformed soldiers emerged. She figured they were probably coming to see the *sołtys*, the head of the village, who lived nearby. Instead, two soldiers walked toward her, saying something. The only German words she could make out were *trinken, trinken*, so she guessed that they were asking her for something to drink.

"*Mleko*," she said to them in Polish before running down to the cellar to retrieve a pot of chilled milk along with an empty cup. The milk that Melania brought back—the good kind, the kind with thick cream on top—was so cold that it could practically be cut with a knife. She placed the pot of milk and the cup on a flat pile of stacked wood before the soldiers. One of the men then pulled out about fifty groszy in coins, put them down on the woodpile, picked up the cup, dipped it deep into the milk, and swallowed the whole cupful.

Melania stared at the money. She had not expected to be paid or to earn fifty groszy, which was good money, considering that her family probably would have just fed the extra milk to their pigs after making butter from the cream. Maybe all the gossip she had heard about the Germans was true: that they were good managers; that they had taken a liking to the mountainous Lemko region; that they would install electricity in the village; that they would provide the farmers with better tools so that she would no longer have to farm with just scythes and rakes; and that with them life would be better than it had been under the Poles.

The two Germans poured themselves a few more cups of milk from the pot and soon were calling out to their friends, "*Kommen Sie! Kommen Sie!*" A few more soldiers came over from the army trucks to join them. When they all finished the milk, Melania signaled that she could bring some more from the cellar, but the soldiers motioned that it was not necessary because their stomachs were already full.

A few days later, with the coins she had earned, Melania bought herself a kerchief. It was a white kerchief that she could wear every day and that would not make her hot by absorbing the sun's rays while she worked in the fields. She tied the kerchief in a way that showed off her long brown braid instead of arranging her hair in a bun and covering it modestly like the village's married women did.

Around this same time, in the middle of Poland, Hitler's eastward-advancing soldiers were arriving at the Narew, Bug, Vistula, and San Rivers, which connected to create a natural north–south boundary dividing the country. From the other direction, Red Army units were approaching. They had invaded Poland from the east on September 17,

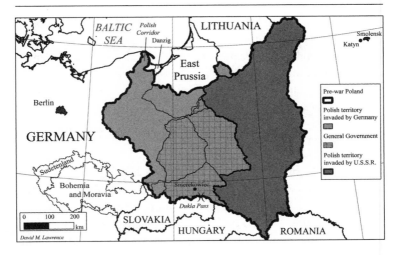

Poland in September 1939

1939, under the secret terms of a nonaggression pact signed by the Soviet and German foreign ministers, Vyacheslav Molotov and Joachim von Ribbentrop. The Soviet Union and Germany had agreed to divide Poland in half at a demarcation line created by the natural boundary of the rivers. They also agreed to reorder their new territories by resettling minority groups and creating more homogeneous populations.

Poland's leaders fled and established a government-in-exile as the Soviets and Nazis completed their defeat of the Second Polish Republic. Hitler annexed Poland's western and northern regions into his Third Reich and turned the rest of the Polish land that Germany had invaded into a colonial state, named the General Government. The Germans now ruled the Lemko region and all those living in it, including the Pyrtej family.

Hitler divided the General Government into four administrative territories: Distrikt Krakau, where the Pyrtej family suddenly found themselves, Distrikt Warschau, Distrikt Lublin, and Distrikt Radom. He then appointed a general governor, Dr. Hans Frank, to administer them. Now that Poland had ceased to exist, German officials took the places of ousted Polish ones in all the government buildings, tax departments, and courts of the bigger towns surrounding Smerekowiec. The

Nazis also recruited local people to go farm in Germany in order to boost the Third Reich's agricultural industry, so Melania began to see lines of young men standing outside the *sołtys*'s house, ready to sign up and make any amount of money in the West. Wagons transported these men to the *Arbeitsamt*, the employment office, in Gorlice, leaving even fewer available suitors in the village than before.

Melania had had suitors before. One young man on whom she was particularly keen—a butcher with a pork business and an impressive eight hundred dollars to his name—had even told her that he wanted to marry her. However, Maria, who had wed Seman when she was only a teenager, insisted that her daughter wait until she was twenty years old to marry, and after Melania explained this to the young man, his family ended up steering him toward a woman from another village with connections in America. There was also a well-off young man from Przysłup whom her parents preferred, but Melania had soured on him when he made fun of a scarf she was wearing.

For the wedding of Maria's younger sister later that fall, Melania made sure to dress in the nicest blouse and skirt she owned. Melania was in the bridal party, so she and the other bridesmaids tried to match the colors of their outfits as best they could. The wedding actually almost did not take place because the Germans arrested the groom-to-be and imprisoned him in Slovakia. He was seized along with another neighbor from Smerekowiec while they were on their way to Gorlice, where, it was rumored, the Germans were raiding stores, many Jewish owned, and leftover goods might be available for the taking. Melania heard that the Germans mistook the men for partisans from the forest before eventually letting them go home from prison weeks later.

The wedding was small, with a Greek Catholic ceremony and a reception attended mostly by family. The guests ate at long tables inside the groom's family's house, sharing bottles of homemade moonshine, plates of bread, cheese, meat, and cabbage, and bowls of chicken broth with potatoes instead of macaroni, which had become a luxury since the start of the war. They danced to a band of musicians playing inside the large barn. Perhaps making up for her lost youth, Maria could not restrain her excitement at the chance to dance, especially at a celebration like her sister's wedding. She loved to be around people and enjoyed drinking an occasional shot of vodka with her circle of female friends. Even when Seman was away selling lumber or came home too tired to change into his Sunday best and go out to a local dance, Maria never hesitated to attend without him, and he never once complained about it.

As the band played, one of the groom's friends, a trim young man with hair that was slicked to one side, walked up to Melania and asked her if she would dance with him. His name was Dmytro Lozyniak. He lived in Smerekowiec too, so Melania had seen him many times, at church on Sundays and at the village cooperative, the local store where he worked. Her family often went to the cooperative to buy or barter goods, like their chickens' eggs for sugar, which was becoming increasingly hard to find. Yet, Melania had never really paid much attention to Dmytro, considering that he was about ten years her senior.

That evening, though, she agreed to a dance with him, which was followed by a second and then a third. By the end of the wedding reception, Dmytro had asked her in Lemko: "*Chy pidesh domiv, chy budesh tu nochuvala?* Are you going home, or are you staying here to sleep tonight?"

"*Ni, ia pidu domiv,*" she answered. "No, I'm going home."

"*Ia khochu z tobom pity,*" he said. "I want to walk with you."

They walked together in the dark, in the chilly mountain air, on the dirt road through Smerekowiec. When they reached Melania's house, Dmytro stopped and declared to her, "*Ia khotiv by sia tobom ozhenyty.* I would like to marry you."

Personally, Melania did not have anything against the idea. She found Dmytro to be smart, handsome, and very kind. "*Ale toto sia ne stane bo ty musysh chekaty.* But that can't happen, because you have to wait," she said, explaining that her parents would not let her get married until she was at least twenty years old, which meant in another three years.

"*Ia pochekam i p'iat,*" he promised her. "I'll even wait five."

Dmytro soon began to visit Melania's house every week, although never by himself. On Sundays he would come with Melania's cousins or some other friends, and they would all sit around, playing cards in a group, talking, or singing. Melania liked that Dmytro had a nice singing voice and was serious and never made fun of anyone, as a lot of other boys in the village did. She did not care that her parents would certainly never approve of him because his family was poorer than hers. Dmytro had six other siblings, including four brothers—Petro, Stefan, Iwan, Roman, Ewa, and Maria—so he could not expect to inherit a lot of land.

Melania's family was considered wealthier by the rest of the village because her father's father, who had died before Melania was born, had made a small side business lending money to people in the region, some of whom used it to travel to the United States so that they could find work there and bring home more money. With the interest that Melania's grandfather made on loans, he had been able to buy dozens of hectares of land for his sons. Still, Melania never felt wealthy when she was required to rake hay, plant grain, and dig up potatoes in the fields.

The Nazi authorities established *kontyngenty*, "quotas" or "levies," in the General Government to make sure that the Germans would have adequate food supplies during the war. Hitler gave orders to take possession of food and other farm products in the occupied territories and to ship them to Germany. The Nazi authorities demanded the quotas from local committees in villages like Smerekowiec, and then the committee members, who had some idea of how much their fellow villagers could afford, carried out the demands. The amount that people were required to give to the kontyngenty depended on factors like the amount of land they owned, the crops they gathered, or the farm animals they possessed. The Pyrtej family found that they were required to give more to the kontyngenty than others in Smerekowiec because they owned more.

Rations were measured in cubic meters—for example, four meters of flax, one meter of grain, ten meters of potatoes—and while the local committee might direct other villagers to contribute half a meter of barley, it would tell the Pyrtej family to contribute maybe three or four meters. Sometimes the committee would even state that the Pyrtej family had still not met their quota, so they would have to scoop out a couple more basketfuls of barley and dump them into a sack to be taken away.

Milk was to be delivered to the kontyngenty once a day, whereas butter was delivered once a week. Melania would carry to the village dairy a pot filled with milk, usually about five liters but sometimes ten, depending on how the cows were producing that day. To churn out one kilogram of butter for the kontyngenty, she needed to milk four cows for seven days straight. The Pyrtej family also gave up a portion of their eggs, chickens (always still alive, so that the hens could lay more eggs), and geese. The family would tell the local committee that they had twenty chickens, even though they really had sixty, and keep the rest out of sight, since none of the committee members ever bothered to come around and count them. The family also gave up a portion of their pigs and sheep and only afterward were allowed to slaughter some of the animals that remained. Butchering meat for personal consumption was no longer allowed without acquiring permission first. The villagers were even required to cut off and give the long hair from their horses' tails, which the Germans apparently needed to create gas masks, Melania learned. She thought the horses all looked ugly with short, spiky tails that would not grow back until the following year.

All the food and other farm products had to be brought to designated collection points. Even the cows were graded from first to fourth class and marked with a special ring on their ears. Every six months or so, Melania would help lead one or two of her family's cows—each of which had a pet name like Krasunia (Pretty Girl) or Zozulia (Cuckoo Bird), and which never received higher than a second- or third-class marker on her ear—all the way over Magura to a collection point in Gorlice. The Germans wanted black cows in particular, Melania noticed, and once turned down her aunt when she tried to offer them two reddish-colored cows in place of a beautiful, big, black one. Handing over your cows meant less milk and butter as well as less manure for your fields, which meant that your farm began to suffer. Yet no one had any choice except to contribute to the kontyngenty, because everyone heard that if they refused, the Gestapo would just come and take what they wanted, leaving the farmers with absolutely nothing. The Nazis drained people, and that was the end of it, Melania thought, likening the Germans who were seizing everything they could from the Lemko region to houseguests who behaved nicely upon arrival but then stole from their host.

The Nazi authorities also passed new laws, defined new crimes, and, month after month, introduced new offenses for which the death penalty was to be imposed. These new offenses included actions against the German government, economic speculation, and Polish soldiers not surrendering as prisoners of war. The Nazi authorities demanded, moreover, that people within the General Government replace their Polish documents with *Kennkarten*, German identification cards. Everyone in the Pyrtej family who was a teenager or older had to apply for a Kennkarte at the local government office in Gorlice. The paperwork required a personal photo, so, with a small camera he owned, Petro snapped and developed the pictures for his family as well as for a few elderly people in Smerekowiec who could not easily have a more professional photo taken. The Kennkarten that the Pyrtej family held in their hands after leaving the local government office were light blue, just like those of all the Ukrainians in the occupied territories. Other ethnicities, such as Poles and Jews, received different colored Kennkarten.

With his diploma from the secondary school for teachers in Krosno, called the *Państwowe Liceum Pedagogiczne*, Petro looked to further his education and career, but the war kept him unemployed at home. In the ensuing chaos, schools were closed, and teachers were not paid. For some time, villagers even compensated the local teacher in Smerekowiec with potatoes, grain, and milk so that she could continue to instruct their children.

Petro had been born in the summer of 1919, right after World War I, when an environment of great conflict between the Polish and Ukrainian nations existed. Following the dissolution of the Austro-Hungarian Empire, Poles and Ukrainians went to war with one another over the border territory known as Galicia. Lemkos of both Ukrainian and Rusyn orientation capitalized on the power vacuum to declare separate autonomous republics in the villages of Komancza and Florynka, respectively, which the Polish government subsequently suppressed. This was a time when the term *Lemko* was spreading in popularity, but many people from Petro's region, including his own parents, still called themselves Rusyns.

Petro had attended the local grammar school in Smerekowiec and then the *Russkaia Bursa*, a Rusyn boarding school in Gorlice, before entering the secondary school for teachers, a Polish school. As he had progressed through the Polish school system, Peter had ignored many an insult about his ethnicity. "*Niech Rusin idzie paść krowy, a nie do szkoły.* A Rusyn should take the cows out to pasture, not go to school," Polish students had said to him. Now within the General Government, however, the Germans were changing the power dynamic between the different nationalities. Throughout Nazi-occupied Poland, the Germans were liquidating the Polish educational system, firing Polish teachers, and revising curriculum topics like geography and history. At the same time, the German authorities were permitting the limited growth of Ukrainian organizations within occupied Poland to counterbalance the Poles. In the spring of 1940, for example, General Governor Hans Frank officially allowed the formation of the Ukrainian Central Committee, which promoted the educational and cultural activity of all Ukrainians in the General Government. The Ukrainian Central Committee, run by Ukrainian nationalists who had fled west from Soviet-controlled territory, was setting up and overseeing Ukrainian educational institutions through its local offices, including in Gorlice. Petro learned that a Ukrainian teachers' seminary would also be opening in the Lemko region, in Krynica, a town best known for its therapeutic mineral springs.

The seminary's objective was to prepare a cadre of Ukrainian elementary school teachers who the Ukrainian Central Committee hoped would promote Ukrainian national consciousness throughout southern Poland. The founders of the seminary chose Krynica as its site largely because the buildings of the town's health resort could be converted into classrooms and dormitories. The seminary offered a four-year program of study as well as a one-year pedagogical course for those who had already finished secondary school. By the start of the first fall semester in 1940, Petro, along with dozens of other students who had passed the seminary's entrance exams, began the yearlong pedagogical course in Krynica.

Melania, having only finished the fourth grade in Smerekowiec, also wanted to study. But her parents told her that school was too expensive and that she did not have time to think about it because somebody needed to stay home to help farm. Melania felt that she could not even attend the German-language classes that one of the Volksdeutsche—people with German roots who lived outside the borders of Germany—began to offer in Smerekowiec in the evenings, because who else would milk the cows? Her father groaned that the price of sending one son off to school was more expensive than paying for three daughters' dowries. So, bestowed with the benefits and duties of the firstborn male, Petro remained one of the very few people from his family as well as his village to pursue a higher education.

Not until just before the summer of 1941 did a German quartermaster come to the Pyrtej house, assessing how much room they had and how close they lived to the road. He informed the family members that a couple of German soldiers and about a half-dozen horses would be quartered with them for a few weeks. The soldiers were instructed to sleep in the little shed that stood by the house—which Petro sometimes used as his room when he came home during school breaks—but the air was so warm that, most nights, they just slept outside on some hay. They used their own military blankets and ate their own military food. They put their horses in the part of the barn where Seman's wagon, now moved outdoors, usually stood and groomed them every day. Melania was impressed with how orderly the soldiers kept everything. They also paid her to do their laundry, lighting their military-issued lamps one night when she was washing their undergarments by hand so that she could see. They were mostly older men with families who showed Melania pictures of their children, explaining that they had been ordered to fight but just wanted to go home to their families.

The German army then sent the soldiers living in the Pyrtej household off to war. On June 22, 1941—just days before Petro received his diploma from the teachers' seminary, written in both German and Ukrainian—Hitler's troops invaded the Soviet Union with a surprise attack code-named Operation Barbarossa, breaking the nonaggression pact with Joseph Stalin. Taking advantage of this opportunity, units of the OUN, the Organization of Ukrainian Nationalists—which had been established more than a decade earlier with the goal of fighting Polish, Russian, or any other foreign control over Ukrainian ethnic territories and creating a Ukrainian state—also followed the German troops into Soviet-occupied Ukraine and declared the establishment of an independent Ukrainian government on June 30. Hitler reacted, however, by turning against the Ukrainian nationalists, ordering the arrest and imprisonment in a concentration camp of Stepan Bandera, the leader of the more radical faction of the OUN, and continuing with his plan to colonize the Soviet territories. Hitler quickly turned the newly conquered region of western Ukraine into the General Government's fifth district, Distrikt Galizien, forcing the Ukrainian independence movement further underground.

German soldiers patrolled Smerekowiec more often. They enforced martial law, and all the villagers had to be in their homes by nine o'clock at night. Guards stood throughout the village and asked people where they were going and why. Sometimes the guards would tease the village boys and joke about whether they were on their way to visit their girlfriends by asking in Polish, "*Panienka? Panienka?* Young lady? Young lady?" One night Dmytro accompanied Melania home after she had been retting flax in the fields, a process of spreading out the cut stems of flax plants to let the evening dew moisten and separate their fibers, which could eventually be spun into linen yarn and then woven. Dmytro and Melania had walked back to her house in the moonlight and were standing by her fence talking when a couple of German officers on horses rode up to them and shined flashlights in their faces. Unafraid, Dmytro said to go ahead and shine them, and the German officers moved on, satisfied that the young couple was not doing anything wrong.

Hitler expected his surprise attack on the Soviet Union to be completed within a few months. However, he underestimated how rapidly the Soviets would mobilize new armies to replace those the Germans destroyed, how many supplies the German army would need to refuel its mobile units, and how slowly the Germans could advance through the sticky mud created by Russian fall rainstorms. By the time the Japanese bombed the U.S. naval base at Pearl Harbor on December 7, 1941, Hitler's troops had reached but not captured their initial targets of Leningrad and Moscow. Unprepared for the freezing cold winter, they suffered through frostbite and outbreaks of typhus.

The Nazi authorities in the General Government, meanwhile, set up ghettos for the Jewish population, often in cities and near centers of transportation. They set up a Jewish ghetto in Gorlice. Melania's friend took her there once when she went with him to town to try to sell some butter and eggs, despite the Nazis' prohibition of such private sales. They were not supposed to enter the ghetto, but Melania's friend went there often anyway to barter his farm products for textiles that the former Jewish shopkeepers had managed to keep. Melania saw how the Jews were forced to wear white armbands marked with a blue Star of David and how Jewish families lived together in cramped quarters, using armoires or other tall furniture to section off the rooms. A few months later, the Nazis liquidated the ghetto, leading hundreds of Jews into the Garbacz forest just outside of Gorlice and executing them. Melania later heard people talk about how they had heard the sounds of shooting and smelled the odors from the bodies.

Dmytro confided in Melania that an acquaintance from a neighboring village had approached him while he was working at the cooperative and asked him to join an underground group that would combat the Nazis. The acquaintance spoke of plans to take over a police department, but Dmytro declined, promising not to give away their plot.

Then one Sunday when Petro was home from his teaching job in another village, Gestapo officers wearing gray uniforms with skull-and-crossbones insignias on their hats appeared in the village. Melania left the house to go to church in the morning, but Petro told her that he would not go with her. Melania, forgetting something, returned a few seconds later, but when she tried to push open the door, Petro was standing behind it, as if hiding or trying to block someone from entering. Melania asked him what he was doing and wondered why he seemed so nervous, but Petro just snapped at her that she should go to church already. Hours later, when Melania got home, she saw that Petro was acting normal again. Only when stories filtered through Smerekowiec about the Gestapo jailing and beating young men from villages such as Kwiatoń, Uście Ruskie, and Hańczowa for attacking German soldiers on Magura did Melania think that perhaps Petro had been hiding the fact that he was working against the Nazis.

Never did Petro talk to his family—who, by and large, stayed out of politics—about how he was a member of the anti-Nazi partisan unit led by Grzegorz Wodzik in the Gwardia Ludowa, the People's Guard. The People's Guard was the military organization of the Polish Workers' Party, a new Polish Communist Party. Petro's code name was Kuczeriawy, meaning "Curly Haired," probably because of his wavy front locks.

The founders of this anti-Nazi unit, including Wodzik, whose code name was Wyścig, meaning "Race" or "Competition," held leftist beliefs based on the ideals of Communism. They supported dairy cooperatives, spoke at rural meetings about how to improve life in the villages, and criticized the lack of available land to farm. They did not trust the

Germans, associating them with memories of Talerhof, a concentration camp built during World War I in which Austro-Hungarian authorities had imprisoned Lemkos and other Ukrainians who felt themselves to be part of the Russian people and promoted the Russian language and culture. They organized self-defense units to protect themselves from the Nazis, attacking Germans to obtain weapons, helping to free Russian soldiers from prisoner-of-war camps, stealing not just butter and eggs but the special rings used to mark the ears of cows meant for the kontyngenty, and persuading friends and fellow villagers to join their cause.

The prolonged fighting in the Soviet Union led to labor shortages in the German war industry, which led the authorities to increase the number of laborers they sent from the General Government to Germany. As Hitler's troops tried for much of the next year to capture the strategic industrial city of Stalingrad, the Germans pressured the village leadership of Smerekowiec to list the names of young men and women who could be forced to work in Germany.

"Run away," Melania's family told her as soon as she got wind that her name was on the list. Melania should go hide in the village of Piorunka about thirty kilometers away, where Petro had taken a job as the director of a school, her family said. While studying at the Ukrainian teachers' seminary, Petro had started seeing a young Lemko woman in the four-year program named Olya Petryszak. Her brother happened to work in Krynica's Arbeitsamt, one of the employment offices where the paperwork to send laborers to Germany was processed. Maybe Olya's brother or his connections could somehow help Melania if someone were to catch her, her family thought.

Melania spent the following winter months living with Petro in Piorunka in housing that the school provided for him before everyone felt that it was safe enough for Dmytro to finally go pick her up. Driving back to Smerekowiec through the snow in a horse-drawn sleigh, Melania and Dmytro agreed that if either one of them were ever to be sent off to Germany, they would quickly get married and go together.

The tide of the war had finally started to turn by the beginning of February 1943, when the exhausted Germans fighting in Stalingrad surrendered to the Soviets. The Red Army proceeded to launch counteroffenses, causing the Germans to withdraw westward. Pressing on toward Poland, Stalin continued to lay the foundation for a Communist government there. He self-righteously severed his remaining relations with the Polish government-in-exile that April after it called on him to explain the discovery of 4,321 bodies in the Katyn Forest near the city of Smolensk and the Germans' correct assertion that the Soviets had executed approximately 15,000 Polish soldiers in detention during the first year of the war. At their conference in Tehran, Iran, that winter, Stalin also pushed the other leaders of the Allied powers, Franklin D. Roosevelt and Winston Churchill, to agree to draw a new Soviet-Polish border farther westward along the Curzon Line—named after the British foreign secretary who had proposed it after World War I—which would delineate Polish and Ukrainian territories based on ethnicity. By January 1, 1944, the new Communist Polish Workers' Party had created a parliamentary-type body, named the National Homeland Council, which was subservient to the Soviet Union. Just days afterward, the Red Army crossed over Poland's prewar boundary.

As the Allied troops were landing in Normandy on D-day, June 6, 1944, Soviet partisans waging guerrilla warfare against Hitler's army were parachuting into the Lemko region. A few weeks later, while walking his horse through the woods on Magura and doing nothing more than admiring the trees, Seman mistakenly came upon about half a dozen of them. The partisans grabbed Seman and hauled him off to their bunker. Fearing for his life, Seman pleaded with them not to kill him, saying that, if they did, someone would come looking for him and would discover them on Magura. Finally, the Soviets let him go, swearing that, if he told anybody about them, they would find his home, burn down his house, and kill his family. For months, Melania's father would not go in the direction of Magura by himself and forbade Melania from taking the cows to the fields beneath the mountain. Whenever she asked why, he would tell her just not to go there.

Morale remained high among the Soviet troops as they continued to advance westward that summer. They carried out a successful offensive, dropping bombs and punching through German lines to capture Lviv. They crossed over the San River and reached the banks of the Vistula River, deflecting German counterattacks while pushing to gain control of the city of Sandomierz in the occupied Polish territories. In the meantime, Stalin and his loyal Polish Communists took further advantage of the Red Army's momentum to proclaim a new governing body in Poland, named the Polish Committee of National Liberation, on July 22, 1944. This governing body stood in direct opposition to the Polish government-in-exile, the leaders of which continued to influence Polish politics from London. One of the first acts of the head of the Polish Committee of National Liberation was to sign a secret document with the Soviet Union on July 27, agreeing to Stalin's terms about a new Soviet-Polish border—on the Curzon Line—after the war.

With the Red Army now approaching the Lemko region, the Germans hastily prepared their defenses and commanded the village head of Smerekowiec to identify young people who could help dig trenches. Melania was working in the middle of a field, pulling out stalks of flax, when German soldiers came and ordered her to go home and gather a change of clothes and some food. She then climbed into a horse-drawn wagon filled with other villagers. They were driven about eighteen kilometers west to the village of Śnietnica, arriving sometime in the evening. That night the German soldiers locked everyone in the school-house, where they slept on the floor next to one another.

Early the following morning, the German soldiers let the villagers out and gave them breakfast—a piece of bread that reminded Melania of a brick as well as black coffee that tasted like it was made from acorns instead of real coffee beans. The soldiers next led them to the trenches, which looked like long, zigzagging ditches, and instructed them to dig deep enough so that a soldier hunched over in the trench could hide his head and wide enough so that a soldier sticking his elbows out could still fit. Melania was able to manage the strenuous digging where there was soil, but whenever she came upon a big rock, one of the men would have to come over and break it up to remove it. Although work in the trenches was exhausting, Melania decided that she preferred it to cooking in the military field kitchen, peeling never-ending potatoes like some of the other women in Śnietnica were forced to do. It seemed harder, she thought, to make sure that the German soldiers always had enough to eat.

Because the Germans were bringing new villagers to Śnietnica every day, the schoolhouse could not hold them all, so the soldiers ordered Melania and others to find shelter elsewhere after their first night. Luckily,

Melania knew of some distant relatives in Śnietnica—her cousin had married someone with family there—so she, along with a few of the girls, went to their house. When they arrived there, though, they saw that the house was full of people who had also been digging trenches. The girls found some space up in the hayloft under the roof of the house, but the biting fleas among the hay kept them from sleeping well.

To anyone who worked in the trenches for ten days in a row, the Germans offered ration coupons that could be used to purchase scarce items like clothing and shoes, Melania heard. For almost five years, clothing had been impossible to buy, so Melania and her mother sewed all the family's shirts, pants, and even underwear out of linen woven from their homemade flax yarn and bleached from the material's natural gray color to white. Seman had once gotten ration coupons after hauling wood for the Germans and bought a pair of shoes for Melania, who usually walked around barefoot, except in the winter. The shoes turned out to be of poor quality, with paper on the inside, and quickly ripped apart.

Melania worked in the trenches for seven days in a row before she started thinking about how she had her own work to do at home and nobody to take care of it for her. Forsaking the ration coupons, she left her relatives' home and snuck away alone one night. She walked the eighteen kilometers back to Smerekowiec, through fields and villages, all by herself in the dark.

As the Red Army moved toward Warsaw in August 1944, Polish resistance fighters belonging to the Armia Krajowa, the Home Army, tried to seize the city. They hoped that their uprising would not only force the German army from Warsaw but also put them in a position to install authorities loyal to the Polish government-in-exile before the pro-Soviet Polish Committee of National Liberation could solidify control. The resistance fighters intended for the uprising to last for only a few days, until the Red Army arrived to fight the Germans. However, the Red Army's advance into Warsaw halted abruptly, and the Soviet leadership chose instead to focus on fighting to the north and the south of the city, abandoning the Polish soldiers and their now-doomed revolt.

Melania began to hear bombs in the distance as the Red Army pressed into the Carpathian Mountains. A German quartermaster returned to the Pyrtej house, but this time with about seven soldiers who needed to be lodged before they could be deployed to the front. The soldiers slept on the floor of the cramped house, bringing hay inside and setting up makeshift beds wherever there was room. They made sure not to sleep in front of the oven so that they would not be in the way whenever Melania or her mother had to cook. During the night, they got up often for night patrol, taking turns on watch every few hours. During the day, their military responsibilities kept them outside of the house. They only returned around mealtimes, with food from the army kitchen in tin lunch boxes that snapped tightly shut and could be heated directly in the oven. Melania would watch as they sat down at the table to eat, using a military-issued utensil that looked like a spoon on one side and a fork on the other. Sometimes she gave them some of the dinner that she had cooked. They seemed, in particular, to like the potato soup she made on Sundays, even though there was no meat in it. The soldiers lodged in the Pyrtej home were quiet, and the family got used to them. Soon, though, the seven of them went off to the front, and rotations of other soldiers took their place. A whole brigade of close to two hundred soldiers, by Melania's guess, was now stationed in Smerekowiec.

Seizing villagers whenever and wherever necessary, the German army continued to send people to the trenches. Melania was forced to go back to Śnietnica numerous times, but she never stayed there more than a couple of days, always managing to run away. The German soldiers did not monitor the villagers as closely when it rained, she learned, so she usually escaped into the woods late on those days. The Germans did not seem to go into the forest at night, so she was pretty sure that, even if they noticed she was missing, they would not try to come after her.

At home during the day, Melania would often take her sewing or other work and climb up into the loft space under the roof to hide from the Germans. She would take along Hania, now eight years old and big enough to accidentally reveal to neighbors or strangers where her big sister was. Hania would cry that she did not want to sit in the loft, that she just wanted to play with her friends, and that she would not tell anybody anything, but Melania still would not let her go outside.

One day, when Melania was eating lunch inside the house with her mother, a couple of German soldiers unexpectedly came to their house.

Melania had nowhere to run; by the time she saw them, the soldiers were already at the window by the front door. While her mother walked over to open the front door, Melania darted into the closet, closing it behind her and not caring that she was standing with her dirty shoes on clothing that was waiting to be ironed.

"*Syn? Córka? Gdzie jest syn, córka?* Son? Daughter? Where is son, daughter?" one of the Germans asked in broken Polish as he entered the house. Melania's mother simply acted as if she did not understand him, shrugging her shoulders and shaking her head. She picked up some eggs that were lying nearby, pretending to think that the men had come for food, and said, "*To, pane?* This, sir?" The German soldiers, rather than searching the house, just took the eggs and left.

At the beginning of September 1944, the Soviets engaged in a battle for the Dukla Pass, a low mountain pass on the border between Poland and Slovakia that sat in the middle of the Lemko region, no more than thirty-five kilometers east of Smerekowiec. The Red Army had not initially planned to cross from Poland to Slovakia through the Dukla Pass but made the detour after Slovak resistance forces appealed for the Soviet Union's help in fighting the occupying Germans. The Red Army's plan was to penetrate into Slovakia through the Dukla Pass within a few days, barraging the Germans with thousands of artillery pieces and mortars backed by air support; but the Germans held them off and countered with their own barrage. The bombs landed on Lemko villages, including Mszana, Tylawa, and Ropianka, as the villagers fled, terrified.

Many villagers fled westward from the bombing through Smere-kowiec. Some had packed whatever belongings they could into their wagons, while others came to the Pyrtej house, hungry and begging for food to eat. The Pyrtej family shared whatever they could—pieces of bread or grain that the refugees could take with them. The Pyrtej family also packed their own suitcases and prepared bread and sacks with grain for themselves in case they also needed to escape the front. They did not know whether the Germans would retreat and, while withdrawing, would force everyone from their homes, so they wanted to be ready.

The front did not pass through the Lemko region quickly, though, because the Germans remained in a standoff with Soviet troops at the Dukla Pass. The Germans commanded higher positions on a number of mountains and pounded the Soviets below with their firepower. Possession of strategic points changed hands several times, but the German army resisted its opponents from trenches and bunkers on the border, setting up minefields as obstacles. Sometimes, when Melania went down into the cellar, she would feel the ground shaking from all the bombing. In the evening, she could see rockets streaking through the air. The Germans patrolling Smerekowiec issued an order for all villagers to cover their windows at night so that the Russian bomber planes would not be able to see the lights and target them.

Finally, after more than a month of fighting, the Soviet troops made a large push through fog and rain and surged across the Dukla Pass. As fighting moved into Slovakia, the German armies began retreating across the border from where they had appeared in 1939. Dozens of German and Soviet tanks clashed in a huge battle south of the pass in an area that Melania and others began to refer to as the Valley of Death. When planes flew overhead toward the combat, Melania could always tell if they were German or Soviet—the German planes always made a heavy "hoo" noise, while the Soviet planes made a ringing sound. "*Stryko yde. Muku nese.* Uncle is coming. He's bringing flour," people in the Lemko region would say now when they saw the Soviet planes. "*Zhytia bude dobre koly Stryko pryde.* Life will be good when Uncle arrives."

Because the colder weather would soon blow in, Melania was busy digging up potatoes when a German soldier once again approached her in the field, this time ordering her to go directly to a wagon that would drive her to the trenches. Melania pleaded that she should at least be allowed to go and get some warm clothes from home. The soldier agreed but said that he would go with her and wait.

No one was in the house when they arrived. After shuffling through her things, Melania pulled out a piece of paper—a German medical report—and handed it to the soldier to read. The report stated that she was pregnant. Only about three months along, she had not told anyone else except Dmytro—the father—and her brother, Petro; but she thought that, if the soldier knew, he would not force her to go dig.

Melania was wrong. She was taken back to Śnietnica to the trenches. Not more than one day passed, though, before Melania escaped home to her family.

Worried that her parents would still not accept Dmytro and allow them to get married, Melania asked Petro to speak with them on her behalf during one of his visits home.

Petro explained to their parents that Dmytro wanted to ask for Melania's hand. He emphasized that now was the time to grant the two of them permission because, with the front approaching, no one knew whether their family would be torn apart. He pointed out that Dmytro was a loyal young man who, over the past four years, had shown a lot of respect to their family and Melania, now twenty-one years old.

Dmytro then approached Melania's parents and asked for their blessing, assuring them that he had two hundred dollars in savings. They agreed to the marriage.

Melania's wedding dress was made from brand-new, light blue silk material that Dmytro bought for her in Slovakia. Like many Lemkos, Dmytro frequently crossed the tightly patrolled border into Slovakia, risking arrest to smuggle back goods that could not be found locally. They would travel in the middle of the night, often when it rained, so that the guards could not hear the leaves rustling as people crept through the beech forest along the border. They would barter fresh butter or cheese for white bread, since the soil and harvests in Slovakia were better. Rather than barter to get the material for Melania, though, Dmytro spent a few of the American dollars that he had been saving.

Melania did not own a sewing machine, so she paid a seamstress to make her wedding dress. She thought it turned out very pretty—it had a modest round neckline, long sleeves, a high waist, and a skirt that flared out down to her calves. She also bought a short veil from a Polish woman whose two daughters had used it, one after the other, for their Holy Communions. The veil would no doubt go on to be borrowed by other young unmarried women whom Melania knew in the village.

On the morning of her October wedding, Melania was all dressed and standing inside her home, ready to leave for the ceremony. Weddings in the Lemko region often took place in the fall, after the gathering of the harvest but before the solemn period of Advent. Dmytro was walking to the Pyrtej house to meet Melania along with the wedding musicians, who would be leading the bridal party and guests in a procession to the church. At that moment, down the street, German soldiers were escorting a group of villagers who looked as if they were being taken to the trenches. The musicians, not wanting to be rounded up, turned around and decided they would not go any farther.

Petro went outside and approached the soldiers, using his fluent German to invite them into the house for breakfast. The family served the soldiers scrambled eggs with bread and butter, along with a few shots of vodka, while Petro asked them to allow the wedding to proceed. Everyone in the house stood by, waiting to see how the Germans would react. *Just let the wedding ceremony take place, and then the Germans can take away both Dmytro and me*, Melania prayed to God. Finally, the German officer in charge—perhaps out of kindness or perhaps because of the alcohol—announced that no one from Smerekowiec would have to go to the trenches that day, and he let all the villagers go.

Soon the musicians were playing a cheerful march as everyone headed down the main road to the village's Greek Catholic church, with its three onion-domed cupolas in the Lemko style. Melania walked in between her two bridesmaids, while Dmytro, wearing a gray suit with a celery-colored shirt and white tie, walked in between his two grooms-men. Stepping over puddles created by the rain the night before, Melania strode in time with the music. Bombs could still be heard in the distance.

After the ceremony, the musicians led the group to Dmytro's house, where a wagon was arranged to carry his few belongings—a brown suit-case filled with his clothes, a big feather pillow that his sister had given him, and an alarm clock—to his new home. Dmytro would now share Melania's bed in his in-laws' house. As they rode in the wagon, Melania and Dmytro passed by the cooperative and came upon a makeshift *szlaban*—a barrier erected by their friends that blocked the newlyweds from passing until they paid off the "toll" with bottles of alcohol. A little farther down the road, they had to pay a second toll.

Once inside the Pyrtej house, the married women performed the tradition of *ochepyny*, taking off Melania's veil and tying her hair into a bun that they covered modestly with a kerchief. The married women sang "*Oi, vchera byla divka*. Oh, yesterday, she was a maiden." The musicians, always the first to be fed so that they could continue playing, then invited guests to dance in the barn, which had a wooden floor and not just dirt, Maria was proud to say. To conceal all the lights, Seman had made sure to cover all the windows in both the house and the barn with thick black paper. The celebration lasted late into the night, and the only German soldiers who came by were there to sneak a taste of the alcohol and take a peek at the reception. One German soldier, noticing little Hania trying to navigate through the room full of celebrating adults, even picked her up and carried her across to her mother.

Melania and her family had no idea that, as the German army and the Red Army continued to battle, the leadership of Communist Poland had secretly agreed to the Soviet Union's idea to exchange their minority populations. On September 9, 1944—just as the Red Army had begun its attack in the Dukla Pass—Nikita Khrushchev, the chairman of the Council of People's Commissars of the Ukrainian Soviet Socialist Republic, traveled to Poland to sign an agreement with Edward Osóbka-Morawski, the leader of the governing Polish Committee of National Liberation, a puppet of Stalin. The Polish Committee of National Liberation consented to the evacuation of all Ukrainians, Belarusians, Russians, and Rusyns who wished to resettle from Poland to the Soviet Union in exchange for the evacuation of all Poles as well as Jews who had been Polish citizens before September 17, 1939, who lived in the western regions of the Soviet Union and wished to resettle to Poland. The Soviet-Polish population exchange was to begin on October 15, 1944, and to end on February 1, 1945, unless both sides agreed to an extension. "The evacuation is voluntary, and, for this reason, force cannot be applied either indirectly or directly," the agreement rules noted.

The population exchange would once and for all end antagonisms between Poland, Ukraine, and other nations by letting minority groups move freely to their "fatherland" and live among their "own countrymen," Osóbka-Morawski claimed. "We believe that, in this way, we will best solve the matter of nationality that has imposed on our lives for centuries," he stated, supporting the idea of one nation-state without any national or ethnic minorities. Past antagonisms included murderous interethnic conflict, such as the killing of forty to sixty thousand Poles by Ukrainians in the Wołyń region in 1943–44 as well as ten to fifteen thousand Ukrainians by Poles in Wołyń, Eastern Galicia, and other parts of Poland from 1943 to 1947.

Ukrainian nationalist groups who continued to fight for the independence of Ukrainian territories denounced and warned against the supposed goals of the population exchange, however. "The Bolsheviks always promise heaven but give hell" and "Stalin wants to evict us from our ancestral land, where our ancestors lived and worked for ages," the Organization of Ukrainian Nationalists' provincial leadership in Poland proclaimed. They threatened that, if Stalin tried to expel the Ukrainian nation, it would respond with all means of resistance. Groups of new Ukrainian partisans, many coming from other parts of Ukraine, gathered on the outskirts of the eastern Lemko region in the isolated woods on the mountain of Bukowe Berdo to receive military training with the hope of joining the OUN's underground military wing, the Ukrainian Insurgent Army (UPA). Focused on the fight in Soviet Ukraine and not believing that it needed to build new divisions in Poland, the OUN-UPA network in Poland was weak at first. Only in the fall of 1944—around the time that the OUN leader Stepan Bandera was released from the Sachsenhausen concentration camp—did the UPA accept these groups of new Ukrainian partisans into its fold, creating the first small battalion in eastern Lemko territory to fight the advancing Soviets and their re-settlement plan.

2

The Reality
of the Soviet-Polish
Population Exchange

The Pyrtej household marked the holiday on December 25, 1944, with a quiet dinner—their Greek Catholic Christmas would be two weeks later, according to the Julian calendar—and then went to bed. A few hours later, their neighbor, Andriy Smereczniak, pounded on their door and woke them up, yelling that the Germans still stationed in Smerekowiec were retreating. The family had better go hide their horse before the soldiers saw the barn and took the horse to escape. Dmytro jumped up, pulled on his clothes, ran to the barn, and led the horse out, with the frost on the ground crunching underfoot. He and Andriy rode their horses on the forest path to Przysłup, which would be hard for any soldiers to reach, since no main road led to the village, and only returned the following night, when they felt it was safe.

For days, the German army retreated past Smerekowiec. What had begun as a strong procession of German military vehicles almost five years earlier, in 1939, now turned into a string of tired soldiers, often propping each other up as they fled. To prevent the Red Army from following them across streams, the Germans were preparing to blow up all the bridges in the village, including the small stone bridge near the Pyrtej house, the family heard.

The family took cover inside, and when the stone bridge finally exploded, the blast's force and noise shattered both windows in the house. The cold winter air immediately seeped inside, so the family tried to warm the house by burning wood in the stove. Dmytro went to the village school, which was closed because of the fighting, to see if he could take glass from the building. Other neighbors did the same. By evening, Dmytro had cut new windows and installed them in the house.

Word soon spread that the Germans had destroyed the wooden bridge at the top of Smerekowiec toward the neighboring village of Gładyszów as well as the newer concrete bridge down past the school. They had also blown up the old sawmill on Magura as they ran away. By the end of the first week of the New Year, all the German soldiers in Smerekowiec seemed to be completely gone.

No sooner had the Germans fled Smerekowiec than a group of Russian partisans walked through the village and entered the Pyrtej home one evening. The leader of the group turned to Seman and asked him, as if they were old friends, what Seman would host them with for the New Year. Recognizing the partisans right away as the ones who had threatened him on Magura a few months earlier, Seman started to apologize that the family did not have much to give.

Melania hurried over to a shelf where the family always stacked loaves of bread, just above another ledge where cups and bowls sat. They would bake five or six loaves and pile them on the shelf so that it was easy to see when the bread was running out and it was time to bake more. She took one remaining loaf off the shelf and brought it over to the leader.

"*Posliednii?*" he asked her in Russian. "Is this the last?"

"*Da, posliednii,*" she answered back. "Yes, the last."

The partisan then pulled out his knife and cut the loaf in two, handing one half back to Melania. He would take only part of the bread to share with his men because he did not want the family telling others that the Russian partisans had taken everything from them, he said before leaving. The Russians had promised that they would bring flour and bread to the people after they won the war, but they were hungry themselves. *Z porozhn'oho ne naliiesh*, Melania thought. You cannot pour from something that is empty.

The Red Army continued to push across Poland, taking over city after city and solidifying Stalin's influence over the Polish leadership. The pro-Soviet Polish Committee of National Liberation was officially transformed in January 1945 into the Provisional Government of the Republic of Poland, which was made responsible for administering all the Polish territories now under Soviet control. Soviet troops forced the Germans to withdraw from Warsaw, allowing the Communists to

Curzon Line
••••••••

Area in box detailed below

POLAND

Zagórzany
Kobylanka
Krosno
Nowy Sącz
Grybów
Gorlice
Klimkówka
Śnietnica
Magura
Gładyszów
Smerekowiec
Piorunka
Zdynia
Ciechania
Czyrna
Wierchomla
Krynica
Tylicz
Iwonicz-Zdrój

Lemko Region

Dukla Pass
Baligród

SLOVAKIA

Dołżyca
Cisna

David M. Lawrence

The Lemko region after World War II

proclaim their liberation of the capital. The Soviets liberated the
Auschwitz concentration camp not long after.

The Polish government-in-exile protested that the Soviet Union was
interfering in Poland's sovereign political affairs. Nonetheless, the leaders
of the Allied powers, Stalin, Roosevelt, and Churchill, had come to the
difficult agreement by the end of their February conference in Yalta that
Poland would remain within the Soviet sphere of influence, with the
condition that free elections of a new Polish parliament would be held.
The three men also agreed to the complete redrawing of Poland's borders,
extending the Soviet Union's boundary with Poland to the Curzon Line
and allowing the Soviet Union to keep the Polish territory it had annexed.
As compensation, the Allies granted Poland some of defeated Germany's
territory. The borders of Poland essentially shifted hundreds of miles
west, with the Lemko region and the Pyrtej home ending up in the
southeastern corner of the country.

Melania went into labor at the very end of February. That same evening, with help from a friend, Dmytro hooked up their horses to the family's wagon and rode toward neighboring Gładyszów to get the local midwife. The retreating Germans had destroyed the bridge leading to Gładyszów, though, and the water in the river was high from all the melting ice and snow. The men chose a section of the river that they knew was shallower and carefully waded across it in the wagon. They did the same on the way back with the midwife. The next morning, March 1, 1945, Melania gave birth at home to a baby girl.

Melania prepared for the baby's christening, which usually took place in the Lemko region within a few weeks of the birth, as superstition held that a woman was not allowed to retrieve water from the well until her child was baptized. Melania decided to name her daughter Maria, after her own mother. When Petro arrived for the christening, though, he suggested that the baby also be given a middle name. Both Petro and Hania thought that the name Nadia would be nice. People in Smerekowiec did not commonly give their children middle names, but the village priest agreed to the idea and christened Melania's daughter Maria Nadia. Melania liked to call her dark- and curly-haired girl Marysia, the diminutive of Maria; however, her family soon took to calling the baby Nadia, and the name stuck.

As the war seemed to be nearing its end, the Pyrtej family began to see Soviet delegations—or agitators, as some of the villagers called them— paying visits to Smerekowiec and speaking of the need for all the Ukrainians in southeastern Poland to resettle to the other side of the new Soviet-Polish border, in Soviet Ukraine. Since the previous fall, tens of thousands of Ukrainians living in Polish counties closer to the border had already been resettled to Soviet Ukraine. Because of the harsh winter, however, the leadership of the Soviet Union and Poland had not succeeded in meeting their original February 1, 1945, deadline for expelling the hundreds of thousands of Ukrainians who still remained throughout southeastern Poland, so they extended the terms of their population exchange agreement. The Polish government soon set up regional offices dealing with resettlement in cities surrounding the Lemko region, including Gorlice, Nowy Sącz, and Krosno.

In some villages, the Soviet delegations would organize meetings, often in the public reading room, to persuade people to sign up to go to the Soviet Union. In some villages, the delegations would walk from house to house, knocking on doors. They promised that Soviet Ukraine was full of fertile land, that it was like a paradise, and that life would be better there. The resettlement campaign became the talk of the region, as people discussed among themselves whether or not they wanted to go. Some of the first Lemkos to sign up were from villages located not too far from the Dukla Pass, like Ciechania, which had been completely destroyed during the war. These Lemkos had no real choice but to resettle because they were left with no homes. The surrounding area was filled with buried mines, which on more than one occasion claimed the life or limb of someone who accidentally stepped on one, and the thawing ground of the nearby "Valley of Death" began to release the stench of decomposing bodies of soldiers who had fought and died there.

In Smerekowiec, one family after another began to sign up to go to Soviet Ukraine, with some saying that they were going *do Rosiï*, to Russia, as people in the village often called all the Soviet territories to the east. Other villagers quickly followed, pouring like honey, Melania would say, into the resettlement offices. The officials responsible for evacuation had been dispatched without enough office supplies, and they practically ran out of paper creating all the resettlement documents, which listed information such as villagers' names, nationality, and amount of property to be left behind. One of Dmytro's brothers-in-law joked that he must have been one of the last people to register, because the only thing the officials had left to write his information on was the inside of some book's cover.

Early on, Seman agreed to sign up his family too. The Soviets came to his house and sat on the wooden benches at his kitchen table, saying that it would be better for his family to resettle from Polish to Ukrainian territory and that everybody in the village was going. While serving in the Austro-Hungarian army during World War I, Seman had ended up a prisoner of war within the Russian Empire for a number of years and come away with the impression that conditions in those territories were good. Based on this experience, he believed what the Russian officials told him and signed up his entire household, including Melania, Dmytro, and baby Nadia.

Petro planned to marry his girlfriend, Olya, as soon as the war was over. Almost four years of courtship had passed since the spring day in 1941 when they first spoke to one another as students at the Ukrainian teachers' seminary in Krynica.

Petro and Olya had noticed each other before that day, but they never had the chance to meet, since their courses were in different buildings. Olya, who walked about seven kilometers every day from her home in Tylicz to Krynica, would arrive at school before her classes started and, while she was waiting, would see Petro walk by. Sometimes she would come to school earlier just to catch a glimpse of him. She found him handsome, with his tall build and wavy hair, and asked some of the other female students if they knew his name. "Petro Pyrtej," one girl told her, although Olya misheard and scribbled down "Pertej" in her notebook. Petro likewise started to notice Olya's pretty hair and fashionable clothing, and he began to search her out. One afternoon after class, seeing her heading home through Krynica, he hurried to catch up with her and introduce himself. As they walked and talked, he spotted a sketchbook that she was holding and convinced her to show him some of her sketches. He teased her flirtatiously about her drawing mistakes, while she just laughed back. Petro escorted Olya all the way to the border of Tylicz, where he said good-bye to her because the sky was turning dark already, and he needed to walk all those kilometers back to his rented room in Krynica.

The rest of that school year was filled with dates to the movies and get-togethers with each other's school friends in Krynica. There were walks around the town, where they would see a Lemko man named Nikifor sitting on a low stone wall, painting churches or other familiar structures. Olya sometimes gave Nikifor, who was poor and mentally challenged, clean sheets of paper on which to paint. She always politely turned down the paintings he offered in return, not knowing that the simple man's works were already gaining notice and that he would one day become a famous primitivist painter.

Even when Petro left Krynica after one year to teach in other villages and became the school director in Piorunka after two years, he would come back to visit Olya. Then, when Olya graduated from the seminary but was sent to teach in the village of Wierchomla, in the opposite direction from Petro, not more than two months elapsed before he arranged to transfer her to the village of Czyrna, close to Piorunka. In Czyrna, Olya faced an empty grammar school that had not been used for years, but she trusted Petro, who told her not to worry and that he would help her as she walked around the village signing up children. Practically every Saturday, he would send one of his students to deliver a bag of groceries to supplement her teacher's salary, which could not even cover a pair of stockings each month. As summer vacation approached, he also gave her a hand with filling out report cards and diplomas.

Petro and Olya discussed marriage, and as a Soviet victory became more certain, Petro went to Tylicz to ask Olya's parents for their blessing. Petro went by himself to the Petryszak household while Olya stayed behind in Czyrna and cried, overcome by the thrill and the gravity of the occasion.

The war in Europe officially ended on May 8, 1945, days after Hitler took his own life in his bunker and American troops captured the former head of the General Government, Hans Frank. Petro and Olya got married on May 17 in Piorunka. Seman, Maria, Hania, and Dmytro all made the trip, transporting as much homemade alcohol, bread, and other food as they could contribute, while Melania stayed home in Smerekowiec to take care of baby Nadia. With the Soviets in control, Olya had been able to get a permit to cross the border into reestablished Czechoslovakia and legally buy a wedding veil and material for her wedding dress. One of her relatives gave her a lilac wedding bouquet as a gift, and one of her bridesmaids arranged for a nearby convent to bake the wedding cake. A Greek Catholic priest conducted the wedding service in Piorunka's Greek Catholic church, while an Orthodox priest volunteered to be deacon for the ceremony. For once, tensions between the followers of the two religions—inflamed when many Lemkos converted to Orthodoxy, considering it their ancestral faith—were ignored out of respect for Petro. A group of Petro's students gathered to sing for Petro and Olya as the newly married couple exited the church. The reception took place in Petro's schoolhouse, where the desks were removed to make enough room for the musicians and dancing.

Petro and Olya lived together in Piorunka for only a couple of weeks. The Polish government was doing whatever it could to increase the number of people who would voluntarily resettle in the Soviet Union, promising relief from paying taxes and opportunities to obtain credit to anyone who would leave. The Petryszak family, along with Olya and Petro, decided to go to Soviet Ukraine. The Polish government—reorganized and renamed the Provisional Government of National Unity to acknowledge the Allies' wishes for a coalition between the Polish Communists and certain government-in-exile members—signed another agreement with Moscow on July 6 encouraging Ukrainians and Rusyns living in Poland to relinquish their Polish citizenship and emigrate by no later than the end of the year. Olya's father trusted the promises of the Soviets, while Olya and Petro trusted Olya's father's judgment. After all, he was a respected man in the community and one of twelve deputies voted to the *rada gminy*, the council that governed the local municipality. He, like Petro's father, had been a prisoner of war in tsarist Russia during World War I and, after returning home, would comment on how honest he had found the people there to be. In Russia, they would hang a slaughtered pig outside without worrying that anybody would steal it, he would tell Olya and her siblings. The Russians were their brothers, he would say. He was sure that there would be good people in the Soviet Union.

Ukrainian nationalist groups in Poland, meanwhile, were trying to convince Lemkos not to trust the Soviet propaganda or to go to the Soviet Union. The Ukrainian Insurgent Army printed and spread around leaflets that read:

> To the inhabitants of the Lemko Region! An injustice is happening to us. . . . They are not allowing us to live on our land. . . . Do not leave the land of your ancestors, which they protected for centuries. . . . Do you want to leave these beautiful mountains and forests? . . . Do you want to leave your churches? . . . Don't allow yourselves to be lied to. . . . Defend your land and your houses. Don't look for happiness elsewhere, and stay here.

The Organization of Ukrainian Nationalists stepped up its information campaign and explained to the people that the population exchange did not have anything to do with improving relations between the Polish and Ukrainian nations; the true reason for resettlement was that the Soviet and Polish governments wanted to destroy the Ukrainian nation collectively. Expulsion of the Ukrainians from their current ancestral lands in southeastern Poland would only lead to their enslavement and slow death in remote areas of the Soviet Union, the OUN said.

Numerous students whom Olya knew from the Ukrainian teachers' seminary agreed with the Ukrainian nationalists and became active in their movement. One of Olya's male classmates from the Lemko village of Ropianka, Mychajlo Fedak, had joined the OUN's iunatstvo, or youth group, when the Germans arrived in Poland, taking on the assignment of organizing a youth network in the western Lemko region. The OUN was cultivating a new type of Lemko, Mychajlo believed, teaching him how to love and fight for the independence of his homeland and to show that the Lemko region was and would be Ukrainian.

At the Ukrainian teachers' seminary, the students had called Mychajlo by the nickname Barabol'ka, meaning "Little Potato," because he was short and round. During their final months at school together, Mychajlo had signed Olya's autograph book with a poem:

> Z dnia-na-den' lysh zhyty,
> Nichym sia ne zhuryty,
> Khloptsiv lysh liubyty,
> Tak staraisia zhyty!!!
>
> Dlia Oli, shchob zhadala kolys'
> takoho iak Barabol'ka
> M. Fedak

> [Just live from day to day,
> Have no worries,
> Only love for boys,
> Try to live in this way!!!
>
> For Olya, so that she might one
> day remember Little Potato
> M. Fedak.]

After graduation, Mychajlo was working as a third-grade teacher in the Lemko village of Mszana when one day he heard the motor of a car outside his classroom. Before he knew what was happening, the classroom door opened, and a Gestapo officer holding a machine gun entered. The officer asked Mychajlo his name and led him to the car, not even giving him the chance to grab his hat or coat. The officer drove him to a building in the town of Jasło, where the Gestapo interrogated him about his membership in the OUN and tortured him every time he denied any involvement with it. Mychajlo's interrogators beat him with rubber sticks, set an attack dog on him, isolated him in a basement as dark as a grave, tied him up, put a mask over his face so that he could not easily breathe, beat him further, and repeated this torment over and over again until they had to carry his damaged body down to his cell. At different times over two months, Mychajlo prayed, panicked, and cried, but he never admitted that he was an OUN member, because he was sure that would result in certain death. Only after he cast doubt on the Gestapo's information, pointing out that maybe it had confused him with another man by the name of Mychajlo Fedak, who also lived in Ropianka, did the Gestapo finally release him. The Gestapo searched for Mychajlo's namesake, but luckily he had already escaped to join the Ukrainian partisans, adopting the pseudonym Sokil, or Falcon. Once beyond the walls of the Gestapo building, Mychajlo swore that he would never allow himself to be caught again, preferring death to jail. He committed himself to a life of underground revolutionary activity, going by the code name Smyrnyi, meaning "Tame" or "Mild."

Olya never crossed paths with Mychajlo again, as he disappeared into the Ukrainian insurgency and rose through its local ranks. After the Soviet-Polish border moved west, the Ukrainian underground reorganized its structure in the spring of 1945. The Ukrainian nationalists referred to the Ukrainian ethnographic lands in Poland that remained beyond the Curzon Line as the Zakerzons'kyi Krai. In the Zakerzons'kyi Krai, the OUN created three administrative divisions, called *okruhy*. *Okruha* 1, which encompassed the entire sub-Carpathian region, was further divided into two *nadraiony*, or superdistricts. One of these superdistricts was called the Beskyd *nadraion* and covered the Lemko region. The Beskyd nadraion was further made up of eight *raiony*, or districts. Smyrnyi became head of the seventh *raion*, while Sokil became head of the eighth. Mychajlo undertook his work within the Ukrainian independence movement with twice the energy as before the Gestapo had caught him. By the summer of 1945, he was organizing *boïvky*, or small battle units, made up of fourteen to sixteen Ukrainian partisans in the western Lemko region.

The OUN and UPA did not find it easy to attract support in the western Lemko region, where they knew that the population looked upon them with apprehension and mistrust. Mychajlo understood the wariness of the Lemkos in his area. He remembered how, during the German occupation, people had at first respected the Ukrainian police—the *sichovyky*, the Lemkos had called them—but the Ukrainian police had not always behaved respectfully in return. He had personally witnessed Ukrainian police officers abusing the locals if they spoke the Lemko vernacular instead of literary Ukrainian or if they didn't use the greeting *"Slava Ukraïni*. Glory to Ukraine." Still, Mychajlo had been educated in the Ukrainian teachers' seminary, many of whose students went on to fight for Ukrainian independence, and he aligned with the Ukrainian partisans who tried to halt the Soviet-Polish population exchange and to discourage Lemkos from leaving their territory.

Among those having second thoughts about resettlement were Dmytro and Melania. They started to hear jokes that villagers were quietly telling, ridiculing the Soviet agitators who promised abundant land and bread—like the joke about the man who attends one of the agitators' informational meeting and asks, "But will we get typhus in the Soviet Union?" only to promptly hear the answer, "Yes, yes, you can take it by the wagonload!"

One by one, Dmytro's brothers had begun to have doubts and back out of resettlement. Only one of his older sisters, Ewa, was still going with her husband. Finally, Dmytro told Melania that if his brothers were not going to leave the Lemko region, then he would not leave either. He complained about how her father had signed them up in the first place. He then went off to try to find an official who could remove his name as well as Melania's and Nadia's from the list of people for evacuation. He brought along a bottle of moonshine and offered it in exchange for the request, hoping that the officials in charge of resettlement had really crossed off their names permanently, he told Melania when he got back home.

All of Smerekowiec might have been ready to leave, but Melania knew that with just one word, "no," her stubborn husband would not change his mind. She agreed to do whatever he wanted. When she broke the news to her parents that she and Dmytro had decided not to go to Soviet Ukraine, Seman was not pleased. "*Tam nashy*. Our people are there," he said in Lemko. "*Shto tu v polakakh budesh sidyv?* What are you going to stay here with the Poles for?"

Petro rushed into the barn soon after arriving in Smerekowiec for a visit in the early summer. His sister Melania sat there crouched on a stool, milking a cow.

"*Choho ne khsesh yty? Choho tu ostaiesh?* Why don't you want to go? Why are you staying here?" he asked in Lemko, demanding to know why she had decided to remain in Smerekowiec.

"*Bo mam malu ditynu. Ia ne pidu z malom ditynom v svit.* Because I have a small child. I am not going out into the world with a small child," she answered before admitting, "*Bo Mytro ne yde. To, ia ne ydu!* Because Dmytro's not going. So, I'm not going!"

Melania was sick of the tension that the decision over evacuating had been causing in her family. For weeks, her parents had been weighing all the arguments. Maria was not sure that she wanted to abandon the home and family life she knew. Seman remained tempted to leave.

Melania ran out of the barn, trailed by her brother, and into the house to find her parents. Once inside, she told her father, emphasizing her last words, "*Nianiu, iak khochete, to ydte z Petrom. Ia vas ne speram. Ale, my . . . ne . . . pideme.* Father, if you want to, then go with Petro. I am not preventing you. But we . . . are not . . . going."

In the end, Melania's mother, who Melania felt always deferred to Petro, surprised her daughter with her decision. "*Ia sia ne rushu odtal nygde. Ia tykh dity ne lyshu.* I am not moving anywhere from here. I will not leave these children," Maria finally said, refusing to part with Melania, Dmytro, and baby Nadia.

Petro came back to Smerekowiec one last time to say good-bye to his family. His mother gave him whatever she could to take on the trip to the Soviet Union, like freshly baked bread to eat and a military blanket—which Melania had bought from the Russian soldiers at the end of the war—to keep him warm.

Petro promised that he would send a letter to his family when he got settled so that they could reconsider whether or not to join him. Even Dmytro agreed that, if life in Soviet Ukraine proved to be better than in the Lemko region, they would follow him.

The Soviet-Polish Population Exchange   47

As Petro stood outside, ready to leave, his mother rushed back into the house. She grabbed a pillow and returned with it under her arm. Not sure if everything she had given him would be enough, she told him to take the pillow too.

Petro, Olya, and the Petryszak family—Olya's parents, two brothers, and two sisters—moved out of their house in Tylicz around late July. They took very little with them beyond a few suitcases and bundles of clothes, a low chest of drawers filled with homemade down comforters, a trunk that Olya's father and Petro built to hold the family's dishes, food for the journey, and three cows. One of the cows was Petro's, a gift from his parents when he started working as a teacher. Petro also took his violin, which he always played at dances. They left behind all the rest of their belongings, including furniture of a kind that nobody else in the village owned. Some villagers might have had a wooden bed, but it was rare to own a dresser and other pieces of furniture made from ash-tree wood, which Olya's grandfather, a deacon, had acquired from a priest and passed down to her mother. They left behind their tin-roofed barn, the biggest in Tylicz, as well as ten hectares of land and dozens of animals, like chickens, that they would not be able to feed during the journey. Poles from the village had already been walking around, assessing the houses that would become available, so the Petryszak family knew that one of their poorer neighbors would likely take anything that remained. They left behind practically everything, certain that the Soviet government would provide whatever they needed.

Still, riding away in their wagon, one of Olga's sisters started to sing, and the family began to cry at the words of her folk song, inspired by generations of other Lemkos who, like them, had departed from home:

> Bud zdrava zemlytse,
> Ydu k Hamerytse,
> Ydu zarablats piniaz'.
> Bud zdrava sestrychko,
> Ne plachte mamychko,
> Yshchy sia vernu dakoly zas.
>
> [Be well, my homeland,
> I am going to America,

I am going to earn money.
Be well, my dear sister,
Don't cry, my dear mother,
I will someday return.]

Before the war, Olya's father had loved to raise horses, feeding them well, hiring one or two people to help take care of them, and even holding friendly competitions with a neighboring Polish priest as to whose animals looked nicer. Olya had always felt proud when her father harnessed his horses to their wagon and the family rode into Krynica for some fair. But the Germans took their horses during the occupation, leaving the Petryszaks with only one unfortunate mare. This mare was now pulling them more than thirty kilometers north, to the train station in the town of Grybów, where residents of Tylicz were supposed to report for resettlement.

Officials in Grybów told the Petryszak family to wait among all the other people until their transportation could be arranged. The authorities were experiencing difficulties and delays because of a lack of trains. The Petryszaks were surprised to see that everyone was being boarded not into regular passenger cars but into covered boxcars with sliding doors, the type used to transport cattle or other freight. Days later, the officials finally assigned the Petryszaks to a boxcar along with two other families from Tylicz, squeezing together about two dozen people. The families divided up the cramped space somehow, each agreeing to settle into a different corner. All of their cows were herded into a separate boxcar. The Petryszaks left their mare and wagon at the station.

Finally, on July 24, 1945, their train pulled out of Grybów and began its journey east. Olya would never forget this day, because July 24 was her name day—a day that she normally would have spent celebrating the feast of the patron saint who shared her name.

On that same date, in Warsaw, the Ministry of Public Administration hosted a delegation of representatives of the Ukrainian population in Poland at a conference, wishing to impress the government's authority upon them so that they would go back to their counties and persuade people to resettle. Among those invited was Michał Doński, one of the former leaders of the Lemko partisans with whom Petro had cooperated in the People's Guard and who now represented the Communist organization called the Peasants' and Workers' Committee of the Lemko Region.

Doński and the delegation members told the ministry that people in their counties had left for Soviet Ukraine because of the wartime destruction of their homes; the declining economy, which could not sustain their families; and the fear that the Polish government would repress national minorities, as it had before the war. Ukrainians and Rusyns still living on their historical lands in Polish provinces west of the Curzon Line did not intend to leave them, however, and considered themselves to be members of the Polish state who deserved to benefit from all the rights guaranteed by its constitution, the delegation said. Peace reigned in the Lemko region, and the people living there had always behaved reasonably toward the Polish nation. All that they asked was that they be free to do such things as to practice their religion, open schools in their language, and have equal access to the economic and political activity of the country.

The Polish government officials at the conference responded that Ukrainians had their own Ukraine—a state in the Soviet Union—and should go there for the good of both the Ukrainian and Polish nations in order to, once and for all, eliminate all the contentious nationality problems. The Polish government did not want any elements that were hostile to the state. Otherwise, although remaining Rusyns and Ukrainians would enjoy the same rights as the Poles, there might be a need for the government to resettle them to other territories within the state, such as for reasons related to land reform following the postwar changes to the borders, the officials claimed. With the delegation members they discussed the possibility of sending the Ukrainian minority to western Poland, for example, saying that they could form their own colonies there.

The train that Petro and his in-laws rode in progressed slowly. It would ride along and then stop at a station, waiting for some amount of time. Then it would start up again, but only to stop at another station, sitting on the tracks for days before the engineer received orders to proceed again. Bringing the engineer a bottle of vodka as a bribe sometimes helped to get the train moving again, the passengers soon learned.

In their boxcar, Petro and the Petryszaks slept wherever they had room—on a makeshift bench fashioned from some of their belongings such as their low chest of drawers and on the floor on their blankets. They fed themselves with the food they had brought. They ate bread, butter, lard, and a lot of *brinza*, a soft white cheese preserved in wooden containers filled with liquid so that it would not dry out and would last a long time. When the train stopped, they were able to take their cows outside to graze and to milk them for something to drink. People could also collect some of the water used to power the train, a steam locomotive, and boil potatoes or other provisions in round metal pots over campfires by their boxcars. There was nowhere to wash oneself or one's clothes properly, though. Very rarely they would stop by a river where they could bathe, and even then people worried that the train might leave without them. Their bathroom was essentially a bucket in the center of the boxcar.

With no real idea of how many kilometers they had left to travel, they rode by Ukrainian village after Ukrainian village destroyed by the war. Once, while their train was stopped somewhere in the middle of the Ukrainian republic, a young woman came up to Petro and Olya. She told them that they should turn back and would regret it if they continued east because of the poverty there. She asked them why they were doing such a stupid thing as to go there, but Petro and Olya just ignored her.

After countless weeks of traveling, cramped and dirty, with no idea exactly where they were being taken, the Petryszak family was told to disembark when the train stopped in the city of Ilovaisk in the Stalino (later to be known as Donetsk) Province. They hauled their suitcases, commode, and cows off the train, while a couple hundred other passengers also clambered out of their boxcars. Everyone waited outside the station—a freight station that predominantly served as a junction for transferring goods—for an official to come tell them where to go. No one came right away, though, so there was nothing more to do than continue to wait. Under the naked sky, the passengers were left to sit on and sleep by their baggage and belongings. One day passed, followed by another, and then another. It rained, and people got wet. Some cried.

Poland after World War II

Some swore. Petro, Olya, and the rest of the family realized that they had made a mistake.

Finally, Soviet officials led by the head of the local kolkhoz, or collective farm, arrived at the station in wagons pulled by cows, since there was a lack of horses after the war. The officials instructed Petro and his in-laws to load up their things and then transported them a few kilometers away to a desolate, one-road village called Fedorivka. The village had been part of a former German colony, one of many established during the Russian Empire by German settlers. Because Fedorivka was in the middle of the steppe, trees and wood were sparse, so most of the buildings were constructed out of stone. Although the stone house in which the Petryszaks were assigned to live was relatively large—with two rooms, the smaller one of which the family let Petro and Olya have for some privacy—its floors were made out of dirt, and it was in worse condition than their home in Tylicz. Besides some metal beds and a table, there was practically no furniture. Right away, the family understood to what kind of "paradise" they had been resettled.

Weeks after Petro's last visit to Smerekowiec, a man showed up at the Pyrtej house. Melania was sitting inside by an open window at a table with baby Nadia while her parents were working outside in the fields. The man, who had served with the Red Army during the war and was making his way back home from the Soviet Union to the Lemko village of Nowica, walked up to the window. Melania did not take long to recognize him. He had worked for a few years in Smerekowiec for a woman whose husband had gone off to America to make some money. He and Melania, both young back then, would see each other at local dances.

The man greeted Melania and tried to hand her a letter through the window, but she insisted that he come inside, so he joined her at the table. She served him bread and butter along with milk to drink while he explained how he happened to have crossed paths with her brother, Petro, while traveling. Waiting on the other side of the Soviet border for paperwork allowing him to go home to the Lemko region, he had been surprised to see Petro at one of the train stations where people being resettled to Ukraine were stopped. Petro immediately asked him if he would carry a note back to Smerekowiec and wrote it while the man waited. Petro practically kissed him when he agreed, the man told Melania before finally handing her the letter and continuing on to Nowica.

Melania showed her parents Petro's note as soon as they came home from the fields. "*Ne rushaite sie z mistsia. Za vsiaku tsinu, zostavaite doma,*" he had written. "Don't leave. At any cost, stay home."

By the end of the summer, the Soviet and Polish governments acknowledged having difficulty finding any individuals who wanted to leave Poland for Soviet Ukraine voluntarily. A representative of the Soviet government responsible for the relocation of the Ukrainian population approached the Polish authorities with the proposal to use the military to push the process forward. On August 22 the Polish authorities called an emergency meeting with the head of the General Staff of the Polish army and commanders of various infantry divisions and decided to direct certain infantries—the Third, Eighth, and Ninth—to complete the resettlement campaign in various Polish districts. In doing so, the Polish authorities were making the decision to abandon the original principle that evacuation was voluntary and force could not be used in favor of a new policy of forcible relocation.

At the same time, the Polish leader Osóbka-Morawski, now the prime minister of Poland's Provisional Government of National Unity, corresponded again with Nikita Khrushchev to discuss extending the population exchange further. Representatives of the Provisional Government of National Unity met with Khrushchev in the capital city of Soviet Ukraine to sign an additional protocol to their original agreement. This protocol prolonged registration for the population exchange until the end of the year, December 31, without stipulating how long it would take to complete the entire relocation campaign.

Because such a great number of Ukrainian families had tried to obtain documents officially changing their religion from Greek Catholic to Roman Catholic, hoping to pass themselves off as Poles so that they would not have to leave, the Ministry of Public Administration additionally decreed that adopting a new faith did not in any way change one's nationality. The Polish authorities also resurrected a decree from before the war, from 1937, citing security as the reason that all Ukrainians and Rusyns had to leave the belt of territories by the border, including the province where the Pyrtej family still lived. This decree would, on the one hand, speed up the evacuation of the Ukrainians and, on the other, liquidate the growing bands of Ukrainian nationalists, the authorities strategized.

The Pyrtej family waited for more news from Petro, but none came. Petro and his in-laws were assigned right away to work at a collective farm named in honor of Molotov, the Soviet foreign minister. The crops surrounding Fedorivka were abundant, but there were not enough people to gather them. Soviet men had gone to war, and, of the fraction who returned, many were crippled. The Petryszak family was healthy and strong, so Petro and his in-laws were sent into the fields, where tall stacks of wheat stood ready for them next to a big threshing machine that separated the wheat seeds from the plant. They were given pitchforks, and their job was to heap the wheat into the thresher. They worked from morning until evening, receiving only about three hundred grams of grain—roughly a cup and a third—per day as compensation.

Petro and Olya, trained to work as schoolteachers, were not used to the hard labor. One day, one of the Soviet administrators came to review the work of the collective farm and saw Olya working with the handle of the pitchfork tucked under her armpit instead of firmly in her two hands. He asked her why she was not holding the pitchfork like she was supposed to, so she silently showed him her palms, swollen with blisters that looked like small plums. Taking pity on her, he ordered her to be transferred to the *horodova bryhada*, the "garden brigade," a section of the collective farm where crops like tomatoes and cucumbers were grown and picked.

Many of the local town women worked in the garden brigade, and Olya watched with surprise as they stole everything they could. On their way to lunch or home in the evening, the women would load their buckets up with fresh tomatoes and cucumbers and cover them with discarded cabbage leaves, pretending to take only scraps to feed their cows. Olya was not accustomed to such stealing. The town women told her not to worry and to take some home too, but she responded that she just could not, so the women grew suspicious of her. Olya quickly realized that there was no place for her in the garden brigade and, after about two weeks, asked to be transferred back to the fields with her family.

Olya could not wait for November 7, the anniversary of the October Revolution. She hoped that they would all have a holiday and be able to rest. On November 6, however, the head of the collective farm gathered everyone and said that it was necessary to celebrate the holiday with work. The Petryszaks heaped wheat into the threshing machine the next day as usual. They worked every day, even Sundays. Near Fedorivka, a house had been turned into a chapel, but Petro and Olya hardly ever attended the church services because they never had any free time. They had practically become slaves, as the Ukrainian nationalists protesting resettlement had predicted.

The piles of grain that the workers harvested often remained in the field overnight before they could be transferred to a storage unit. The administrators of the collective farm assigned workers to guard the grain, but this did not stop people from sneaking around in the dark and stealing it.

One fall night, Petro was scheduled to watch over the grain, so he told his father-in-law to come and take some. For all their exhausting work, the Petryszak family did not have enough food. The Soviets had promised those resettled from Poland the same amount of land as they had left behind, but they had not given Petro and his in-laws any land on which to grow their own crops. From the grain allotted to the family, they could barely bake enough bread for one meal a day. On top of that, the local flour tasted bitter. The milk that their cows produced also tasted bitter because the only thing that the animals could eat was acrid grass on a hill by their house. As their cows got thinner and thinner, one of Olya's brothers, a butcher, slaughtered them for food one by one. With his head in his hands, Petro sat and sobbed when his cow, the last to be slaughtered, was killed, since it represented the last living thing he had from home. Petro had already had to trade his beloved violin with someone for a needed watch.

Olya's father did not want to come and take the grain from Petro, but he agreed to so that the family would have something to eat. He brought a sack with him, which Petro filled, and started to carry the grain home along a path lined with trees and bushes. Halfway there, as the leaves rustled in the night wind, he thought he heard someone behind him. He panicked and, not knowing what to do, tossed the sack and ran off. Flustered and agitated by the time he walked into the house, he told his family that he had never stolen before and would not start now. He would rather be hungry than steal, he said.

The winter was bitterly cold in Fedorivka. Brick stoves, with a covered hole in the top where coal was inserted, heated the old German houses in the village. The collective farm did not give any coal to Petro and his in-laws, however, so they had to make do by burning dried sunflower stalks.

Located nearby was a small coal mine from which a train with coal-filled freight cars would ride along the edge of Fedorivka in the early evenings. Petro learned from other men to go to a particular spot on the railroad tracks where there was an incline and the train moved uphill more slowly. At this spot, the men would jump onto the train, climb atop a freight car, kick chunks of coal on the ground, and then jump off to gather and take home the coal to burn in their stoves. Once, Petro kicked a particularly large piece of coal off the freight car, but it fell under the wheel, got stuck, and blocked the train from moving. The conductor stopped the train while Petro, terrified, jumped off and ran away. He only came back for the coal after the train was out of sight.

Reports began to reach the Polish Ministry of Public Administration that Lemko families relocated to the Soviet Union were starting to return to Poland illegally. These Lemkos often returned on transportation meant for Poles who were being simultaneously expelled. The reports recommended that, because those evacuated to the Soviet Union had officially lost their Polish citizenship and were now considered foreigners, any returnees should be detained by public security organs, forcibly transported back to the border, and handed over as Soviet citizens to the Soviet border guards.

Tens of thousands of Lemkos had already been resettled, but those who remained in Poland were resisting, the reports stated. Thus, to prevent disagreements with Lemkos who argued that they should not be evacuated because they were a separate nationality from Ukrainians, local Polish authorities began to include the word "Łemkowie"—Lemkos in Polish—on announcements ordering Ukrainians and Rusyns to evacuate.

The reports to the ministry additionally noted that the Ukrainian nationalists fighting both the Polish and Soviet governments were only aggravating the resistance of the Lemkos. The OUN, for example, had issued orders to treat anyone who signed up for resettlement, even under pressure, as a traitor. Likewise, the UPA had issued orders to destroy re-settlement offices and to burn villages that Ukrainians had been forced to leave so that Polish authorities could not resettle Poles there after-ward. "Let the fires burn after us, let no one rejoice in our work, and let the enemy know that we will not freely give ourselves to be destroyed," the UPA's orders stated, ending with the slogan "*Slava Ukraïni! Heroyam Slava!* Glory to Ukraine! Glory to the Heroes!"

Having still not succeeded in completing the population exchange, the Polish and Soviet governments signed another additional protocol to their agreement on December 14, 1945, prolonging the end of the reloca-tion campaign until June 15 the following year. In areas such as the eastern Lemko region, the Polish army beat and killed people who tried to oppose the order to evacuate.

Overworked and half-starved, Petro and Olya, meanwhile, decided that they also wanted to leave the collective farm. They had heard that some of their family members and friends from the Lemko region were now living in the western part of Soviet Ukraine. Through gossip and letters they found out that, while they had been resettled all the way east, others had been resettled to the western part of the republic. At least there they could be closer to the Carpathian Mountains as well as the forests and rivers they had grown up with instead of on the dry steppe.

Petro and Olya went to the head of the collective farm and requested that he grant them the necessary paperwork to leave. They even tried to persuade him by giving him a down comforter that Olya had gotten as a wedding present. But he refused, so during the first months of 1946, Petro and Olya planned to escape west. Olya's siblings would come with them, but her parents, feeling themselves too old to flee, would stay in Fedorivka until Petro and Olya sent word that they were all safe.

It was a mild spring night in 1946 when Petro, Olya, and her siblings slipped quietly out of the collective farm. They escaped with even fewer suitcases than they had brought east, leaving behind items like the dishes that Petro and Olya had received when they first got married. They walked in the dark to the train station in Ilovaisk and waited there until the early morning, when a train finally pulled in. Quickly, they climbed into an uncovered railroad car and sat on the floor among the dusty piles of coal that it was carrying.

As the train rode westward and stopped at different stations, people in dirty and ripped clothing climbed into their railroad car. The people were from the Moldavian Soviet Socialist Republic and were fleeing a famine caused by a recent drought and strict Soviet quota demands. At a later station, however, a couple of officials policing the train ordered all the poor Moldovans to get out of the railroad car. One of the officials then pointed toward Petro and Olya's group, huddled together, and asked his colleague what to do about them. Olya heard the colleague say that they looked like a bunch of artists—although she was not sure what gave him that impression—and just to leave them alone.

Days later, the train rode into the western Ukrainian city of Ternopil, not far from where Petro knew that his mother's sister, resettled to Soviet Ukraine at the same time as the Petryszak family, was now living. Petro, Olya, and her siblings climbed out from the coal car, with their white teeth shining against the black soot that completely covered them. They washed the best they could with cold water at a hydrant nearby. Locating Petro's aunt a few kilometers away in the city of Petrykiv, they squeezed into her small apartment for a few days, even celebrating Easter Sunday with her. They soon realized, though, that no work or housing existed for them in Petrykiv and that they would need to move on.

They traveled farther, sometimes by foot, sometimes hitching a ride by car, more than seventy-five kilometers south to the city of Monastyryska, where they found many Lemkos who had been resettled from Krynica. With no real industries in Monastyryska, however, the city offered even fewer job prospects, so they continued farther west.

They next headed toward the city of Stanisławów, where Olya had a distant aunt. On the way, they reached a river whose flooded waters had recently washed away the bridge, which was replaced by a wide wooden plank with a handrail. Gripping the handrail with one hand and the hand of the person next to them with the other, they all cautiously traversed the shaky plank, all the while praying for God's help not to fall into the rough moving water just below.

Once in Stanisławów, Olya and Petro slept on the floor of her aunt's one-room apartment. Some other Lemkos living not far away put up Olya's siblings. After two weeks, Olya's aunt was able to find Olya and Petro a place of their own—an apartment with one room and a kitchen that was owned by a Polish woman who was being expelled to Poland through the population exchange. Olya and Petro wished to return home to the Lemko region, but they knew they would never be allowed to cross the border. They sent word to Olya's parents to make their way to Stanisławów, where they would all try to rebuild their lives.

With the June 15 deadline to complete the population exchange fast approaching, the Polish authorities gave orders to increase the speed of evacuation and the number of families forced to leave Poland for the Soviet Union each day. Divisions of the Polish army—now organized into a special operational group called GO Rzeszów that was tasked with helping to finish the resettlement—were ordered in the spring of 1946 to evacuate hundreds more households from the Lemko region. Lemkos from the town of Krosno wrote a letter on March 29 to the deputy prime minister of the Provisional Government of National Unity, Władysław Gomułka, who had hidden during the war in Gorlice in a bakery then run by the Lemko activist Michał Doński. They asked him to help put an end to the inhumane expulsion of the Lemkos, saying that they were good, peaceful, and loyal and that, just as flowers in nature were not one color but a variety, people were not and could not be of one type, faith, or language. Gomułka then wrote a letter on April 19 to a representative of the Ministry of Public Administration, saying that he had received news about the forcible resettlement of the Lemkos, who were favorably disposed toward Poland, and that a command should be issued strictly prohibiting the use of any coercion during their evacuation. No evidence suggests that such a command was issued, however.

Rumors spread across the western Lemko region that the Polish army was hauling off people from villages not far from Smerekowiec, such as Gładyszów and Krzywa, to the train stations. Melania and her family heard that the Polish army was taking whomever it could find, so people were starting to run off into the woods to avoid being seized. Dmytro likewise loaded up a few days' worth of food, clothes, and other necessities into his wagon, took one of the cows for milk, and went off to hide in the woods. He and Melania decided that it would be best for baby Nadia if Melania stayed at home with her; but after a few days, Melania got scared that the authorities would come to their house and force the rest of her family to evacuate, separating them from Dmytro for good. She took Nadia and joined Dmytro in the spot in the woods about two kilometers away where the family knew he would be. The three of them slept covered by feather comforters in a tent. Luckily, the weather was warm, and it did not rain. Every couple of days, Dmytro would run back to their house to get some cooked food—potatoes, cabbage, macaroni, or whatever else Maria had been able to cook for them. Melania only regretted that she had recently stopped breastfeeding Nadia, who was a little over one year old, because they now had to worry about giving her cow's milk from a bottle. Dmytro would also find out from Maria and Seman what they had heard about the Polish army. Nobody had any idea when the soldiers might decide to come to Smere-kowiec to take people away. Before long, though, Dmytro learned that the situation had quieted down, so he and Melania decided that they had had enough of the woods and would go home to face whatever would be.

According to the results that the Polish and Soviet officials announced at the end of the population exchange, approximately 482,107 individuals had been resettled from Poland to the U.S.S.R., totaling 96.8 percent of the expected number. Some Polish officials argued that trying to force the remaining Ukrainian population to leave, including Lemkos who were loyal citizens, might push them to join the bands of Ukrainian nationalists. Other officials, however, returned to the idea of sending the remaining Ukrainians to the former German territories that Poland had acquired after the war. One final report, which was marked secret, to the General Staff of the Polish army that July 1946 stated:

> Ludność ukraińską (Łemkowie), co do której istnieją jakiekolwiek zastrzeżenia dotyczące ich loyalności i możliwości zagrożenia bezpieczeństwa, spokoju i porządku publicznego, należy bezwzględnie wysiedlić pojedyńczymi rodzinami, a nie w grupach, na tereny zachodnie, gdzie z biegiem czasu ludność ta uległaby asymilacji.

> [The Ukrainian (Lemko) population about whom there exists any reservations concerning their loyalty and possibility to threaten security, peace, and public order should be ruthlessly relocated by individual family, not in groups, to the western territories, where over the course of time the population will succumb to assimilation.]

The Polish government was still looking for another way to deal with the remainder of its Ukrainian minority.

Damian Howansky and his wife-to-be, Fotyna Szewczyk, before World War II. Photo provided by Stefan Howansky.

Damian Howansky (*left*) with his father, Emilian, and son Stefan in Żdynia. Photo provided by Stefan Howansky.

Maria, Seman, Petro, and Hania Pyrtej in the Lemko region. Photo provided by Melania Pyrtej Lozyniak.

Melania, Maria, Hania, Petro, and Seman Pyrtej in the Lemko region. Photo provided by Melania Pyrtej Lozyniak.

Petro Pyrtej. Photo provided by Olya Petryszak Pyrtej.

Melania Pyrtej. Photo provided by Melania Pyrtej Lozyniak.

Melania Pyrtej (*third from left, wearing embroidered white blouse*) in the Lemko region. Photo proided by Melania Pyrtej Lozyniak.

Melania Pyrtej (*second from right*) with German soldiers quartered in Smerekowiec during World War II. Photo provided by Melania Pyrtej Lozyniak.

The Pyrtej house in Smerekowiec. Photo provided by Melania Pyrtej Lozyniak.

The Greek Catholic church in Smerekowiec. Photo provided by Melania Pyrtej Lozyniak.

Dmytro Lozyniak. Photo provided by Olya Petryszak Pyrtej.

Melania Pyrtej and Dmytro Lozyniak while courting. Photo provided by Melania Pyrtej Lozyniak.

Petro Pyrtej (*third row, standing fourth from left*) at the Russkaia Bursa, a Rusyn boarding school, in Gorlice. Photo provided by Olya Petryszak Pyrtej.

Petro Pyrtej (*second row, sitting far right*) while studying at the Państwowe Liceum Pedagogiczne, a secondary school for teachers in Krosno. Photo provided by Olya Petryszak Pyrtej.

Petro Pyrtej (*front row, second from right*) marching while at the Ukrainian teachers' seminary in Krynica. Photo provided by Olya Petryszak Pyrtej.

Olya Petryszak (*front row, third from left*) marching while at the Ukrainian teachers' seminary in Krynica. Photo provided by Olya Petryszak Pyrtej.

Olya Petryszak (*second woman standing from left*) and Mychajlo Fedak (*front row, sitting third from both right and left*) at the Ukrainian teachers' seminary in Krynica. Photo provided by Olya Petryszak Pyrtej.

Mychajlo Fedak, known as Smyrnyi (*third from right*), in the Organization of Ukrainian Nationalists, with Sokil (*fourth from right*). Photo provided by Myroslava Anna Diakun.

Olya Petryszak (*far left*) with her parents and siblings in Tylicz. Photo provided by Olya Petryszak Pyrtej.

Wedding photo of Olya Petryszak and Petro Pyrtej. Photo provided by Olya Petryszak Pyrtej.

Potwierdzenie

Niniejszym pozwierdzam odbior doprowadzonych w dniu dzis
iejszym do tut. Obozu Pracy z polecenia W.U.B.P. w Krakowie ze stacji Oswiecim, niżej wymienionych więzniw "U"

Dziamba Piotr   ur.13. 5.1908
Pawczyk Antoni   10. 3.97

Jaworzno dnia 30.6.47   /-/ Swieszek M.

Wojskowa Prokuratura
    Rejonowa
  w Krakowie.

dnia_____

ZAŚWIADCZENIE Nr. 01336

Zaświadcza się, że Ob. *Kapitula*
Dawid s. *Aleksandra*
urodz. *ho xr. 1911.* w *Łodynia*
został w dniu dzisiejszym zwolniony z aresztu,
z dyspozycji Wojskowej Prokuratury Rejonowej
w Krakowie. — Wymieniony(a) udaje się do
miejsca swego stałego zamieszkania.

Prokura

m. p.

(—) Karliner ppłk.

Wojskowa Prokuratura
Rejonowa
w Krakowie.

dnia *5. i 48*

ZAŚWIADCZENIE Nr. 01281

Zaświadcza się, że Ob. *Howański*
Damian s. Emiljana
urodz. *14. VII 1913* w *Żołyni*
został w dniu dzisiejszym zwolniony z aresztu,
z dyspozycji Wojskowej Prokuratury Rejonowej
w Krakowie. — Wymieniony(a) udaje się do
miejsca swego stałego zamieszkania.

Document releasing Damian Howansky from the Central Labor Camp in Jaworzno.
Provided by Stefan Howansky.

Top left: Document showing the arrival of Piotr Dziamba and Antoni Pawczyk at the
Central Labor Camp in Jaworzno. From Instytut Pamięci Narodowej archives in Kraków,
075/8, tom. 2, k. 33, 84 i 85. Provided by Eugeniusz Misiło, Archiwum Ukraińskie w
Warszawie.

Bottom left: Document releasing Pawel Kapitula from the Central Labor Camp in Jaworzno.
Provided by Steve Kapitula.

PAŃSTWOWY URZĄD REPATRIACYJNY POW. ODZIAŁ w _Gorlice_ 13

Zagorzany, dnia _17.06_ 1947

Karta przesiedleńcza Nr. _17964_

Ob. _Kapitula Maria_ _____ urodz. w roku _1917_
    (imię i nazwisko, imię ojca)

mieszkaniec miasta _____—_____ wsi _Zolynia_ Nr. d. _109_

gmina _Sekowa_ powiat _Gorlice_ _____ przesiedla się na

inne miejsce zamieszkania. Wraz z nim przesiedlają się następujący

członkowie jego rodziny.

Lp.	Imię i nazwisko	Rok ur.	Stosunek pokr. do głowy rodziny	Uwaga
1.	Kapitula Anna	1939	córka	
2.	— „ — Parasha	1944	— „ —	
3.				
4.				
5.				
6.				
7.				
8.				

Przesiedlający się*):

    a) zabiera ze sobą: koni _1_, krów _1_, trzody chlewnej _1_,

    kóz _1_, owiec _____, oraz następujący inwentarz martwy

    b) pozostawił: ziemi ogółem _3_ ha.

    w tym użytków rolnych _6_ ha.

    dom mieszkalny (jaki) _____

    stodoła _1_ obora _1_

    szopa* _1_ chlew _1_

    (miejsce na pieczęć)

Podpis przesiedleńca _____

Podpis sporządzającego _____

*) Niepotrzebne skreślić. _Kapitula Marja_

Relocation card of Pawel Kapitula's family while he was imprisoned in the Central Labor Camp in Jaworzno. Provided by Steve Kapitula.

Melania and Dmytro Lozyniak holding daughters Julia and Nadia, respectively, in Troska. Photo provided by Melania Pyrtej Lozyniak.

Dmytro Lozyniak (*center*) with brothers Iwan and Roman and children Julia and Petro in western Poland. Photo provided by Melania Pyrtej Lozyniak.

Dmytro Lozyniak working in the PGR, the state-run collective farm. Photo provided by Melania Pyrtej Lozyniak.

Hania Pyrtej. Photo provided by Melania Pyrtej Lozyniak.

Hania Pyrtej. Photo provided by Anna Pyrtej Lozyniak.

Melania and her family saying good-bye in Jarogniewice before leaving for the United States. Photo provided by Melania Pyrtej Lozyniak.

Top left: Petro Pyrtej teaching in Ukraine. Photo provided by Olya Petryszak Pyrtej.

Bottom left: A rare picture of Hania, Petro, and Melania all together during one of Petro's visits to western Poland. Photo provided by Melania Pyrtej Lozyniak.

Melania and Dmytro Lozyniak with their children on the day they immigrated to the United States. Photo provided by Melania Pyrtej Lozyniak.

3

Operation Vistula

The Solution
to the "Ukrainian Problem"

Melania was sitting on the edge of her bed in Smerekowiec one warm August night in 1946, saying her evening prayers before climbing underneath the covers, when pounding on the window outside startled her. Almost three months pregnant with her second child, Melania was the only adult at home and was watching over baby Nadia and ten-year-old Hania. Dmytro and her parents had traveled to another Lemko village that afternoon to help tend the land of a relative who had gone to work in America. They were supposed to bring back some hay in the process and would not be home for another couple of days.

"Open up!" an unfamiliar male voice ordered in Ukrainian, "*My svoï.* We're your people."

Hands shaking, Melania pulled open one of the side-hinged windows a crack, allowing it to swing inward just enough so that she could peek at the person outside. A big, bright moon shined on about half a dozen men, and Melania saw that they were Ukrainian partisans. The activity of the Ukrainian Insurgent Army was getting stronger in the western Lemko region, although Melania had never really understood how its members expected to create an independent Ukraine there when they had not been successful in creating one on the territory that was now Soviet Ukraine. Because of the UPA soldiers' strategy of moving around the woods in small groups, the Polish government was having trouble combating them. By night the Ukrainian partisans would come to the villages in search of food, clothing, weapons, and ammunition, and by day the Polish army would punish any villagers who gave the insurgents anything. There was no peace, Melania felt.

"I can't open up. I'm home alone," she called back to the men.

The partisan who spoke was unrelenting, though. "If you don't let us in, we'll burn down your house," he threatened.

Melania had no doubt that they would follow through on their threat in order to get what they needed. She had heard how, only a few weeks earlier, to drive off the Poles expelled from Soviet Ukraine, the UPA had set fire to about nineteen houses in the nearby village of Klimkówka that had belonged to Lemkos before they were resettled to Soviet Ukraine. Even from Smerekowiec, Melania had seen from afar how the fire lit up the night sky over Klimkówka. Trying to disrupt the resettlement process, a battle unit led by the Ukrainian partisan Smyrnyi had also recently torched houses in Łabowa before any Poles could move into them as well as destroyed the village's post office and police station, killing and wounding several Polish officers and policemen. Active in the local area and numbering over one hundred people, Smyrnyi's battle unit had, additionally, ransacked provisions while raiding a cooperative store in Gładyszów and seized some horses while ambushing Polish civilians in wagons who were carrying the former property of Ukrainian villagers from Kotań.

Melania, still clad in her light cotton nightshirt, stumbled through the dark and grabbed a kerosene lamp hanging in the middle of the room. Because her hands were still trembling hard, she passed the lamp with matches through the open window, asking the partisans to light it for her so that she could see what she was doing inside. They passed it back to her, and she hung it back up before unlocking and opening the front door. A couple of UPA soldiers rushed in and began assessing the home's contents.

"Who else is in the house?" one of the partisans asked.

Melania pointed out Hania and Nadia, both still sleeping in separate corners of the room, and then sat down on the bed next to her daughter's crib. The partisan, with his rifle hanging from his shoulder, took the position of standing watch over her.

"If you scream or try to run away, we'll shoot you," he warned.

The thought that the UPA would kill her and that Nadia would be left with no mother suddenly hit Melania, who felt as if she could not breathe.

"Well, if you kill me, then make sure also to kill my child so that she's not left an orphan," she blurted out. Her entire body was trembling so hard that she worried she might miscarry.

Another UPA soldier took the kerosene lamp and shined the light on the bed across the room where Hania had fallen asleep on top of a khaki army blanket after a day of running around. He looked as if he wanted to take the blanket back to the woods, but the partisan watching over Melania told him not to because he might end up waking the girl and causing her to cry.

Melania did not move as the UPA soldiers began to raid her home. She heard a pig squealing and realized that they were also ransacking the animal pen outside.

"What, they're killing the pig?" she asked. The first partisan nodded.

Melania watched as her guard, who was dressed in civilian clothing and looked about twenty-five years old, paced around the room, rifling through any papers that he saw lying about. He walked up to a red pepper plant on the windowsill, picked off all of its small, ripe peppers, and put them in a pocket in his bag. Melania said nothing.

A UPA soldier then called Melania out of the main room of the house into a storage area. She walked in to find the cabinet that her family kept in the storage area emptied of all their winter clothes, including sheepskin coats and woolen trousers, as well as the small sum of money that they had hidden in it. Draped over the shoulder of the partisan and tied together by their shoestrings was a new pair of leather shoes that Dmytro had cobbled for Wasyl. Melania could not stop herself from asking the UPA soldier how he could take shoes from a poor farmhand who had worked so hard and given so many years of his service to her family.

"*Ia sluzhu Ukraïni*," he responded. "I serve Ukraine."

Returning to the main room of the house, Melania saw that the UPA had also started raiding her family's two tall armoires while she had been in the storage area. The room now smelled of paint fumes from a container of varnish in the armoire that had tipped over. The partisans had removed all the family's clothing from the armoires, including Melania's undergarments, probably for some of their female soldiers. Among the men's dress shirts that one of the UPA soldiers was carrying, Melania noticed the celery-colored shirt that Dmytro had worn on their wedding day.

"No, you can't take that one. It's my husband's wedding shirt," she protested. Without an argument, the partisan handed it back to her.

Before leaving, the partisan asked her whether there was a rubber raincoat anywhere in the house. No, she said, her husband had taken it along with him when he left that afternoon, just in case it rained while they were gone.

Peering out the window, Melania watched as the moonlit figures of the half dozen or so men shoved their loot into large bags. Several of the men hoisted the bags onto their shoulders, while two of them carried a big, long stick from which the Pyrtejs' slaughtered pig, tied by its ankles, hung upside down.

Melania sat quietly in the house for what seemed like a long time before her mind began to wander and she began to worry that maybe the partisans had left a kerosene lamp burning somewhere and a fire would accidentally break out. She dared to walk around outside the house, checking everything and inspecting what had been taken. Although tears streamed down her face, she did not allow herself to break down crying. What good would that do, since she had nobody to cry to? She found a pair of shoes that remained in the storage area and hid them, afraid that someone else might come back to take them. Finally, she climbed back into bed, but she could not sleep.

The next morning, after Melania got up to milk the cows, Polish soldiers walked up to the Pyrtej house. They instructed Melania to go work in the fields of villagers who had been evacuated to Soviet Ukraine in order to rake hay for the Polish army's horses.

"*Gdzie byliście w nocy kiedy byli partyzanci? W nocy was nie było,*" Melania said to them in Polish with mixed sarcasm and bitterness. "Where were you last night when the partisans were here? At night you weren't around."

She pointed to the remains of her pig—intestines, ears, and snout—that the Ukrainian partisans had left lying on the ground.

The Polish government tried to renew the population exchange agreement with the Soviet Union and to continue expelling the Ukrainian minority; however, Soviet officials rejected a further official extension.

Operation Vistula

By the fall of 1946, the Polish authorities acknowledged that their additional attempts at resettlement to the Soviet Union—resulting in some reports of the Polish army beating people—had not been successful. They liquidated GO Rzeszów, the special operational group of the Polish army in charge of expulsion.

The idea of sending the remaining Ukrainian minority to other territories within the state then resurfaced when a brigade general by the name of Ostap Steca wrote a report about the activities of the Ukrainian as well as Polish underground that November. Steca was born in the Lemko village of Komańcza but had served in the Red Army before his superiors transferred him back to Poland and eventually made him head of the Third Operational Department of the General Staff of the Polish army. His report stated that because the Ukrainian and mixed population was still helping the UPA and could not be trusted to be loyal to the Polish state, the Polish government should send this population to the so-called Ziemie Odzyskane—the Recovered Territories, as the Polish Communists now referred to the western and northern territories that the Allied powers had taken from Germany and granted to Poland after World War II. Steca's report concluded: "The security of the border territory, in which bands of UPA operate with the support of the mixed Polish-Ukrainian population, can be resolved primarily by forced resettlement to the Recovered Territories into one well-defined area under the permanent control of security organs." Steca sent his report, marked secret, to various government ministers, including the deputy prime minister of the Provisional Government of National Unity, Władysław Gomułka, and the president of the National Homeland Council, Bolesław Bierut.

The Polish government's attention shifted over the winter months, though, from fighting the UPA to eliminating opposition candidates to the parliamentary elections, which had been promised at the Yalta Conference and were to be held on January 19, 1947. The Polish Communists controlled these elections in the end, claiming that they were free and democratic, despite preventing hundreds of thousands of former Polish resistance members from voting and falsifying the final results. The power of the Communists in Poland solidified as a new parliament called the Legislative Sejm officially replaced the National Homeland Council and the Provisional Government of National Unity was dissolved. That February, Bolesław Bierut was elected president.

At the end of January, Polish army divisions in southeastern Poland got an order stating that the resettlement of the Ukrainian population had not achieved a 100 percent result and that they were required to compile information about the number of Ukrainians who remained. A month later, on February 20, a deputy chief of the General Staff of the Polish army, Gen. Stefan Mossor, submitted a strictly confidential report to the minister of national defense, Michał Żymierski, reiterating that the remaining Ukrainian population was a base for the bands of UPA members and a danger with regard to future irredentism — the annexation of territories by another state on the grounds of common ethnicity. Poland had already lost much territory to the Soviet Union, including major cities like Lwów and Wilno, and wanted to prevent losing any more on its southeastern border to the Ukrainian independence movement. Mossor wrote:

> Ponieważ Związek Radziecki nie przyjmuje już obecnie tych ludzi, wydaje się rzeczą konieczną aby na wiosnę przeprowadzić energiczną akcję przesiedlenia tych ludzi pojedyńczymi rodzinami w rozproszeniu na całych Ziemiach Odzyskanych, gdzie szybko się zasymilują.

> [Since the Soviet Union will no longer accept these people, it seems necessary in the spring to conduct a vigorous campaign relocating these people by individual families, scattering them all over the Recovered Territories, where they will quickly assimilate.]

He estimated, incorrectly it would turn out, that the Polish government would need to relocate approximately 4,876 Ukrainian families, or 20,306 people, to the Recovered Territories, including 367 families, or 2,258 people, from the county of Gorlice, where the Pyrtej family lived.

On March 27 both Mossor and Steca attended a meeting with the Commission of State Security, where the relocation of the Ukrainians continued to be discussed. During this meeting, government ministers agreed to raise this issue further at higher levels. The very next day, though, events in the mountains of southeastern Poland would provide the Polish government with the pretext needed to remove the rest of the Ukrainian minority, including those living in the Lemko region, and to disperse them throughout western and northern Poland.

The morning of March 28, Gen. Karol Świerczewski, the Polish vice minister of national defense, was traveling through southeastern Poland, conducting inspections of military troops in the area, official reports of his activities would later explain. He had inspected the Thirty-Fourth Infantry regiment in the village of Baligród and now wanted to review the border troops in the village of Cisna. His subordinates informed him that the road from Baligród to Cisna was dangerous; months earlier, Polish soldiers had destroyed one of the Ukrainian Insurgent Army's underground hospitals in the area, and the Ukrainian insurgents would probably be looking for a chance to counterattack. The general brushed off any risk, however, saying that it was also possible for a brick to fall on someone's head in Warsaw.

Sometime around 9:00 a.m., Świerczewski set out for Cisna in a three-vehicle caravan, guarded by his security detail. The first military vehicle transported sixteen soldiers and four officers armed with sub-machine guns, rifles, and grenades; the second transported Świerczewski along with four officers and four soldiers with machine guns; and the third transported nineteen soldiers from the Thirty-Fourth Infantry regiment as well as two more officers carrying additional rifles and machine guns. Unfortunately, no commander was designated in charge of security in the case of an attack, nor was any group instructed on special emergency tactics or given responsibility for directly protecting the general.

After driving only about three hundred meters from Baligród, the first vehicle exhibited radiator problems, slowing the caravan down. Świerczewski told one of the lieutenant colonels from that vehicle to move into his and the other two drivers to pass it so that it could follow behind them. Less than two kilometers farther down the road, though, the faulty automobile's engine overheated, so one of the officers decided to return to Baligród to exchange it for a better one. Now only a two-vehicle caravan made up of thirty-three military men, including the drivers, continued on to Cisna.

At around 9:30 a.m., the vehicles were about seven kilometers south of Baligród when, suddenly, heavy automatic gunfire from a steep, tree-covered hill to their right began striking the two vehicles. Świerczewski ordered his driver to go faster as they sped over a bridge that crossed a brook. About forty meters beyond the bridge, he then ordered his driver to stop and everyone to get out. With some of the officers, Świerczewski took up a position in a ditch along the right side of the road, and, after some time, to get to a better spot, they moved through the ditch toward the brook and waded across it.

The second vehicle, meanwhile, stopped about twenty meters before the bridge, where the rest of the security detail got out. Świerczewski passed orders to them to spread out along the length of the right side of the road and to shoot uphill. The soldiers carried out this command, firing dozens of meters upward, but return fire struck and killed one of their lieutenants as well as Świerczewski's driver as he tried to go back to their vehicle and turn it around in the direction of Baligród.

The attackers, who had been waiting on the hill, seemed to have the advantage in terms of surprise and amount of firepower. Their line of fire extended five or six hundred meters across the hills that overlooked the road and the rest of the area. Exploiting their position, they began to advance.

Świerczewski, fearing encirclement, now gave the order to create a line of defense on the other side of the road, along the brook. To do this, his group needed to run through the heavy fire of the attackers. Świerczewski crossed over to the left side of the road and took up a new position between two gullies by the brook. At some point when the general straightened up, however, he was shot in the stomach.

Hearing Świerczewski call out that he had been wounded, one of the colonels ordered some officers to run over to him. The general, in the meantime, left his position between the gullies, moved in the direction of the brook, and descended into its riverbed, at which point he was shot again, this time in the left shoulder. The first officer who reached Świerczewski lifted him under his shoulders and, with the help of three other men, led him thirty or so meters along the riverbed. When they reached a spot where there was no gunfire, they came out onto the bank and tried to wrap the general's wounds. The shots were fatal, though.

Minutes later, the third vehicle, which had been exchanged in Baligród, finally arrived with an additional security detail. As it drove up, the fire from the attackers died down. By the time the vehicle stopped and soldiers jumped out, the attackers ceased their shooting completely and retreated. Officers carried the dead body of Świerczewski to one of the

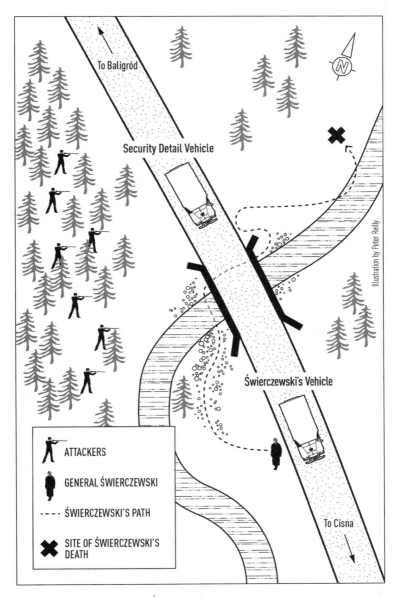

To Baligród

Security Detail Vehicle

Illustration by Peter Reilly

Świerczewski's Vehicle

ATTACKERS

GENERAL ŚWIERCZEWSKI

ŚWIERCZEWSKI'S PATH

SITE OF ŚWIERCZEWSKI'S DEATH

To Cisna

The assassination of Gen. Karol Świerczewski. Illustrated by Peter Reilly.

vehicles and drove it back to Baligród. Soldiers searched the hills where the attackers had stood, but without enough ammunition, they did not try to follow after them. Nobody could say for sure, but the entire fight seemed to have lasted between forty-five minutes to an hour. Because none of the participants were caught, neither could anybody say for sure who had conducted the attack—which division of the UPA or whether another diversionist group had made it look as if the UPA was responsible—and what the reasoning behind the assassination had been, the official reports would admit.

Hello, hello, we are broadcasting an announcement from the Ministry of National Defense," the radio broadcaster at Polish Radio said over the airwaves during that evening's news program. "On March 28th of this year at about ten o'clock in the morning, during official inspections, from insidious bullets of the Ukrainian fascists of the UPA, on the Sanok–Baligród road, died the general-colonel Karol Świerczewski—the deputy vice minister of national defense, the former commander of the Second Army, the hero of battles for the Lusatian Neisse. The remains will be transported by plane to Warsaw. The date of the funeral will, additionally, be announced."

The Polish authorities were officially blaming the Ukrainian partisans for Świerczewski's death.

On March 29 the Politburo of the Central Committee of the Polish Workers' Party, including such members as Gomułka and Bierut, called a meeting in Warsaw to discuss the death of Świerczewski. They discussed issues such as the general's funeral and possible tributes to him, such as a monument or street in his name. They also decided to take repressive actions against the entire Ukrainian population. According to the notes of their meeting, they resolved (1) to relocate Ukrainians and mixed families to the Recovered Territories as quickly as possible without creating mass groups and not closer than one hundred kilometers from the border, (2) to coordinate the relocation operation with the governments of the Soviet Union and Czechoslovakia, and (3) to develop data about the Ukrainian population in Poland and to prepare a relocation plan.

In the weeks that followed, Minister of National Defense Żymierski sent letters to his counterparts in the Soviet Union and Czechoslovakia, stating that the government of Poland had definitively decided to cleanse its border territories of the bands of the UPA and that, at the same time, the Ukrainian population would be evacuated from those territories to the northwestern regions, where they would be distributed as rural settlers. Writing of his fear that unwanted elements would penetrate into the territories of the Soviet Union and Czechoslovakia, the Polish minister requested that their mutual borders be closed for a period of time lasting approximately two months.

The Politburo members also designated a special operational group commanded by General Mossor to carry out the forced relocation operation. The relocation plan that Mossor presented to the Politburo members that April, marked secret, was codenamed Akcja Wschód, or Operation East, and began with the words "Once and for all to solve the Ukrainian problem in Poland." Within a day or two, though, the code name of the relocation plan changed to Akcja Wisła, or Operation Vistula, and Mossor's operational group became GO Wisła. The new name was appropriate given that the Vistula River, the longest river in Poland, stretched from its source in the Carpathian Mountains all the way north through the Recovered Territories and into the Baltic Sea. Operation Vistula was to be kept in the strictest confidence within the military before it was carried out, and officers were to avoid conversations with the population about it, according to orders from commanders of the Polish army to their divisions.

At the beginning of spring, a light snow fell in Smerekowiec, which was not uncommon in the mountains at this time of year. Dmytro decided that he would take advantage of the weather by transporting some manure on a sleigh out to the fields. His horses would be able to pull the sleigh of manure over the snow to parts of the hilly fields that a wagon could not reach when the weather was warmer because its wheels would sink into the moist soil. Dmytro would then pile the manure, which was collected from the pigs, cows, and horses, in mounds across the fields, where it would wait to be spread as crop fertilizer once the ground thawed.

Dmytro ate lunch with Melania and was about to get to work when a Polish soldier stopped at the Pyrtej house for a cigarette and a chat. The soldier, wearing the uniform and buzzed haircut required of the Polish army, looked about twenty years old. He had come by the house before and seemed to have developed a fondness for Nadia. The two-year-old, unafraid, would pass items like her toys or a pillow to the soldier and play with him just as she would with her own father. Melania—who now was the mother of two, having given birth in February to a second daughter, Julia—watched the soldier pick up and bounce Nadia and wondered if he happened to have any children of his own. Dmytro chatted with the soldier for a few minutes and then excused himself to ride out to the fields.

"*Niech pan tak ciężko ne pracuje, bo państwo tutaj i tak nie będą,*" the soldier told him in Polish. "Don't work too hard, sir, because you're not going to stay here in any case."

Paying no attention to the comment, Dmytro just waved his hand and went about his business.

Melania, though, asked, "*A gdzie pójdziemy?* And where will we go?"

The soldier just shook his head and responded, "*Nam nie wolno powiedzić, bo to jest tajemnica wojskowa.* We're not allowed to say, because it's a military secret."

Mossor, as commander of Operation Vistula, sent a telegram to Minister of National Defense Żymierski on April 28, 1947, exactly one month after the death of Świerczewski. The telegram read: "I am reporting that today at 4:00 a.m. the relocation operation of the Ukrainian population began on the whole territory of the operational group."

Divisions of the Polish army had entered the first of the Ukrainian villages and informed the Ukrainian inhabitants that they would be relocated. Within only a few hours, the Ukrainians packed what they could and were transported to designated train stations, where they were loaded into cattle cars to be shipped across the country. The first transport, number R-10, left the Szczawne-Kulaszne station in the southeastern county of Sanok on April 29, carrying 268 people, and traveled all the way north by the Baltic Sea, arriving at the station in Słupsk about four days later. The Polish authorities made sure to note for the commanders responsible for this transport that its passengers consisted mostly of Greek Catholic Ukrainians from a village called Dołżyca, which had been a base for bands of the UPA. Therefore, the people should not all be relocated in one area but divided into groups of no more than three or four families so that they could not organize any sort of resistance. All the relocated Ukrainians were supposed to be spread out in small groups to the maximum degree possible.

Operation Vistula was well under way by the time the governments of Poland and Soviet Ukraine signed their final protocol affirming that the two sides had completed their population exchange in an atmosphere of mutual understanding and agreement. Other villages were being relocated and other transports were leaving train stations for the Recovered Territories day after day, week after week.

Returning from a visit to Gorlice one day, the Pyrtejs' neighbor, Andriy Smereczniak, came by and told Melania that he had seen loads of people with their cattle and packed wagons, but he had been too timid to ask what was going on. He and Melania wondered aloud what this mass of people had been doing. Maybe they were just more ethnic Poles who had come from Soviet Ukraine, they guessed hopefully.

Secret or not, news eventually reached the Pyrtej household that they would have no choice but to leave their home and move to another part of Poland. The entire Ukrainian population had to leave, supposedly as retribution for the death of General Świerczewski and helping the UPA, they heard. The Polish army was moving the Ukrainians village by village, beginning with those closer to the Soviet-Polish border and moving westward. Polish families would be allowed to stay.

Seman and Maria did not believe the news at first. Seman objected to the idea that the Polish government could force him to leave the land where his parents and other ancestors had lived and that now belonged to him. The Pyrtej family complained in private that they had done nothing wrong and had been good, taxpaying citizens, so they should be allowed to stay if they wanted to. But nobody dared to argue with the Polish authorities.

At the beginning of the summer, the village head of Smerekowiec started walking around saying that anybody with a wagon or a horse had to go help evacuate the neighboring villages. Even people with only one horse had to hook it up to someone else's cart. So every day, including Sundays, Dmytro hitched his two horses to his wagon, rode to nearby villages like Gładyszów, Krzywa, Małastów, Radocyna, and Regetów, and transported the villagers and their belongings to a train station about thirty kilometers north in the town of Zagórzany. One day after he returned home, he told Melania about a woman from Regetów who was going to leave behind many of her things, like some nice stone mugs for drinking milk, but a Polish soldier told her that she had better take as much as she could and helped her to pack everything into a wagon. The soldier said not to leave anything, because she would need it all. Dmytro warned Melania that they should get ready for the same fate.

Other stories made their way to Melania's ears in the meantime. She heard about young women who quickly married Poles, knowing that members of Polish families could stay, and about people who tried to obtain *metryky*, certificates of baptism, from the Roman Catholic Church to provide evidence that they were Polish. She heard about a distant family member in the village of Skwirtne whose husband was evacuated without her while she was visiting her mother in another village and who rushed off to the Zagórzany train station to find him. And she heard about a family friend who transported a newborn calf in a wheelbarrow from the village of Żdynia to Zagórzany, a trip that took hours, because he did not have a wagon to carry it in and refused to leave it behind.

Melania's family, luckier than others because they had days rather than hours to prepare, started to pack their things. Melania and Maria knew that there would not be enough room in the wagon for the family's two tall armoires, so they transferred whatever clothing the family had — including Melania's wedding dress — into horizontal wooden storage chests. They took the icon of the Virgin Mary off the wall and, to prevent it from breaking, wrapped it in some of the clothes and placed it inside a chest. They left the rest of the decorative pictures on the walls, deeming them unnecessary to take along. Dmytro built extra wooden crates for the potatoes and other provisions that the family would bring to eat during the trip. He dumped rye, oats, and flour into bags that were a meter long and not too big to be carried. Not having brought much into the household when he and Melania got married, he packed whatever his father-in-law told him to, not always without argument between the two men. Seman sold one of his pigs and two of his cows to some Poles who came through Smerekowiec knowing that they could buy items for a low price from people being relocated. Seman figured that he was better off selling them, because he had heard that the Polish army was confiscating some farm animals from people, which later turned out just to be a rumor. He killed a second of his pigs and salted and dried the pork, while Melania and Maria baked bread for the trip. The family also gathered and bundled piles of hay to be used to feed the farm animals that they would keep while traveling—two horses, a goat, and two cows, one of which was pregnant and would soon give birth.

The Pyrtejs hoped that, wherever they were going, there would be fields where they could grow food, so they packed enough provisions to last them until they could get settled. Perhaps they would not even be relocated for that long and would be allowed to return to Smerekowiec, villagers started to gossip. Clinging to the idea that the family might be able to come back in time to gather their crops in the fall, Melania, like many of her neighbors, continued to work in the fields every day.

Melania had never before seen the young Polish soldiers who came to her family's door at around six o'clock on a sunny morning in June. "*Powiadomiamy Panstwa, że wywłaszczamy z tego domu.* Ladies and gentlemen, we are informing you that we are expropriating this house," the soldiers said, notifying the family members that they were required to evacuate that day.

Melania was surprised by the politeness of the soldiers, who had all been instructed earlier to avoid negative treatment of the population so as not to provoke further support for the Ukrainian nationalists fighting the relocation operation. The two soldiers did not say much, though, before moving from house to house in Smerekowiec. Nobody needed them to. After weeks of witnessing the relocation operation, everyone in the village knew the local procedure by now. The residents of Smerekowiec would be dispatched to neighboring Gładyszów, the center of the *gmina*, or district, which was already evacuated. They would stay there for a few nights before continuing all the way to a gathering point at the Zagórzany train station, where the Polish authorities could closely supervise everyone awaiting relocation.

Melania and her family rushed around the house, tending to last-minute details. Melania packed away the linens, pots, and pans that they had still been using. She chased down the chickens, shoving about ten of them into cages. Soon all the family's boxes, sacks, and other belongings were ready to be piled into their two wagons. A bed was loaded into each wagon. Melania also made sure that they took her hay-filled mattress, something that hardly anybody in Smerekowiec owned or could afford.

She decided not to bring the cradle, however, since Nadia never let her put baby Julia into it and demanded to be rocked every time Melania tried, so Julia had just learned to sleep on the bed. Among the other furniture that they could not fit in their wagons and left inside the house was an additional bed frame, a cabinet for dishes, a table that could not be taken apart, and a number of long benches that lined the walls of the main room. Half of their basement also remained stocked with potatoes because they could not carry all of them. Melania did not worry much about abandoning these things, though, because she had heard the Polish soldiers say that the villagers could find furniture in the former German territories where they were being sent.

Next, Melania dressed Nadia and Julia for the road. She made sure to slip the rest of the two hundred American dollars that Dmytro had saved into a pocket she had sewn in the blanket in which she carried Julia. Dmytro, in the meantime, led the two horses from the stable and hitched them to one of the wagons so that they could both help pull the heavy load. The family decided that Dmytro would transport Seman, Maria, and Hania the four kilometers to Gładyszów in the first wagon while Melania waited in the house with their daughters for him to come back for the second wagon. Wasyl used the opportunity to take the cows and goat out to pasture in Smerekowiec one last time.

The first wagon had departed by the afternoon. Arriving in Gładyszów, Dmytro and his in-laws decided to park in a barn that had belonged to a family member of Maria's who had been evacuated in the weeks before. The barn was close to the road and large enough to fit at least four wagons. Dmytro unhitched the horses and rode back to Smerekowiec on one of them while leading the other. When he returned, Wasyl finished milking the farm animals, pouring their milk into portable ceramic containers and putting them in the second wagon. He tied the cows and goat to the wagon so that they could not run away as Dmytro harnessed the two horses to it.

Melania took one last look inside the house to make sure that they had not forgotten anything important. She made the Eastern rite sign of the cross—touching in turn her head, chest, right shoulder, and left shoulder—and whispered, "*Bozhe, provody nas.* God, guide us." Once her family left, they would have no way to let her brother, Petro, know where they had gone, since they still had no address for him. She fought back tears and a lump in her throat as she turned away from their home.

Melania, Dmytro, and their daughters rode away slowly in their second wagon, while Wasyl walked beside them, tending to the goat and cows. The pregnant cow's midsection, rust-colored like the rest of her coat, swayed as she wobbled along. Only a couple of other wagons rode in front of and behind them, since the hundreds of residents evacuated from Smerekowiec—including Dmytro's parents, who traveled with his brothers, and Melania's maternal grandmother, who traveled with some of her uncles and aunts—had left the village at different times of day, whenever they were ready. The traffic thickened once they got closer to Gładyszów, as wagons rolled in from other villages from all different directions.

Melania and her family lived in the barn in Gładyszów while waiting for further instructions. They slept on piles of hay covered with their own sheets and blankets in the warm summer weather and carried water from a well to wash and cook for themselves. Melania was not surprised to hear from one of the local boys that, right after they left Smerekowiec, some Polish soldiers found all the leftover potatoes in their basement and carried sacks of them off to the army kitchen.

After a few days, the family's pregnant cow went into labor and gave birth to a calf that was rust colored like its mother. Soon after that, the Polish army gave orders for everyone to move north to the train station in Zagórzany. Dmytro again transported Seman, Maria, and Hania in the first wagon, pulled by the two horses, over and past the Magura mountain peak this time. Their wagon followed a long line of others, halting whenever the wagons in front of them did. Wasyl started walking with the cows and goat, making stops when necessary to let the animals graze by the side of the road and singing aloud as he always did to pass the time in the fields. Melania stayed behind in the barn with Nadia, Julia, the second wagon, and the newborn calf, waiting for Dmytro to shuttle back once more. She watched as other wagons and people came through the barn, parked temporarily, and left.

Melania stayed busy taking care of her girls, cleaning their dirty hands, feet, faces, and bottoms, while the calf lay a few meters away.

When she turned around to check on the calf, though, she saw that a man was trying to carry it off. She yelled at him, asking him what he thought he was doing and saying that it was her family's calf. The man, also a villager from Smerekowiec, tried to defend himself by claiming that he had just seen the calf lying there and did not know that it belonged to anyone. Melania responded that he should just focus on his own things. She figured he had seen the Pyrtej family's first wagon leave and had thought that he could profit by taking and selling the calf to someone. That night, Melania slept in the barn with Julia on one side, Nadia on the other, and the calf close by.

The following day, as Melania continued to wait, she let Nadia run around barefoot, since the child had kicked off the new leather shoes that Dmytro had recently made for her. Melania had put the shoes down on one of the family's boxes while she watched over Nadia and breastfed Julia. However, when it was time to put the new shoes back on Nadia, they were gone. Someone had taken them, although Melania did not know who. When Dmytro finally returned, Melania had to dress Nadia in an old, worn-out pair of shoes that she dug out from their things so that Nadia would have something to wear on her feet for the rest of the trip.

Dmytro drove the family to an area near the train station in Zagórzany that had once been a park but was now trampled by the thousands of people, animals, and wagons that had already passed through. Smerekowiec was one of the last villages to be relocated from the county of Gorlice. Polish soldiers patrolled everywhere. The soldiers told those being evacuated to wait before they could board one of the trains heading daily to the Recovered Territories, so at least fifty or sixty wagons stood around at once. With two small children, Melania did nothing but stay, day and night, by the wagons of all her family members. Even when the summer rain started to fall, all she could do was help pull an arched canvas cover—like the ones Americans in the Old West had used—over the top of one of their wagons and sit underneath it with her daughters, waiting for the bad weather to pass. The rain created mud all over the ground of the former park, and Melania did not want to walk around in the horrible mess.

After a couple of days in Zagórzany, Seman got restless and decided to take a walk to Gorlice, where people were still allowed to go to buy goods. Wasyl also left to wander around the waiting area. Not long afterward, some Polish soldiers approached Melania in her wagon, describing Wasyl, who they knew was wearing a hat, and asked her where they could find him.

"*My chcemy go trochę pobić*," the soldiers told her in Polish. "We want to beat him up a little."

"*Dlaczego? Za co?*" Melania cried. "Why? What for?"

The men snickered and assured her that they were just looking for Wasyl because they had heard him singing some Polish military songs and wanted him to entertain the soldiers while they all ate. Eventually, they found Wasyl, who, ever the type to like an audience, went to their army kitchen and sang for the men. In return, they rewarded him with a large pot of soup with meat, beans, and macaroni, which he brought back to the wagons. Melania and the rest of the family ate their fill of the soup and still had enough left over to feed their cows.

Seman, however, did not return to the wagons until later that evening, guarded by some other Polish officers. Instead of going to Gorlice, he had walked the thirty kilometers all the way back to Smerekowiec. He had not been able to resist an urge to see his home again, even though there was an official order banning all those being relocated from returning to their villages. He had wandered from room to room in his house, finding in a cabinet a ceramic container filled with milk, which he just put on the table for someone else to scavenge. On his way back to Zagórzany, some Polish officers arrested him.

Seman had tried to talk his way out of the situation. He said that he had just forgotten something in his house and was on his way back to the train station. He said that he was no threat to the Polish army and that, when the war had broken out, he had even saved a Polish soldier—Stanisław Barszcz was his name—from the Nazis.

As destiny would have it, Stanisław Barszcz was still an active soldier in the area, and the Polish officers were able to summon him to confirm Seman's story. After more than seven and a half years, Seman and Stanisław came face to face again, and, this time, Stanisław was the one to help. Confirming that the Pyrtej family had hid and fed him during the war, Stanisław persuaded the Polish officers to let Seman go. Later, Stanisław also paid a visit to the family at the train station in Zagórzany and tried to allay their worries about the relocation, saying that there would still be nice potatoes waiting to be dug up when, eventually, they were allowed to move back to Smerekowiec. He told Melania that it was too bad that he had never been able to introduce her to his Polish cousin and marry them off, because then she might have had a chance to stay.

As they continued to wait by the train station, Melania and her family received coffee and bread as well as hay for their cows from the Polish army. Unsure of how difficult the trip to the Recovered Territories would be, they decided to sell their newborn calf to a Polish man. They cooked their own meals, using a three-legged metal stand with a circular rim that Dmytro had welded together before leaving Smerekowiec. Melania would build a fire underneath the stand's legs and slide a pot into the rim to boil water over the heat. With the hot water, she could also wash Dmytro's shirts or her daughters' cloth diapers in a wooden basin.

Then, one morning, days after they had been forced to leave their homes, Melania and her family were told to prepare to board the train. Dmytro and Seman had to report to a stand at the station where the Polish authorities in charge of relocation told them to sign up for one of several towns, with names such as Nowa Sól and Milicz, to which the villagers of Smerekowiec were being sent. Not knowing the difference between any of the towns or even exactly where they were located on a map, Dmytro's brothers and parents randomly selected Nowa Sól. Dmytro followed their lead, as did Seman and some of the other members of the extended Pyrtej family. However, Melania's relatives on her mother's side, including Melania's maternal grandmother, selected Milicz because they had other family members and friends who were arbitrarily signing up to go there. The train to Milicz, located approximately 140 kilometers from Nowa Sól, was not scheduled to leave until the following day, so Melania's grandmother and mother said a tearful good-bye, not sure when they would see each other next.

Melania's family was assigned to the third or so boxcar in a long line of boxcars behind the locomotive. They loaded up all their belongings, including their two horses, two cows, goat, and cages of chickens. Melania thought it good that they did not own any sheep, which would have just jumped all over the boxcar. Her family laid blankets on top of their long wooden storage chests so that Seman, Maria, and Hania could use them as beds. Melania, Dmytro, and their daughters would sleep together on the mattress, set on top of sacks of grain, while Wasyl occupied a cot. Once everything was unloaded from their two wagons, the men were told to disassemble them and pile all of the wagon parts into uncovered boxcars at the end of the train.

Melania realized that she and her family actually had better conditions than many of the people on board the train. Officially, two families were assigned to each boxcar. However, she, Dmytro, and their children counted as one unit, while her parents, Hania, and Wasyl counted as a second unit, even though they all came from the same household. Their boxcar was, therefore, not as crowded as it could have been. Melania had seen families of eight, for example, crammed in with yet more people.

Finally, on June 26, 1947, their train, marked R-253, pulled out of Zagórzany carrying 209 people, 41 horses, 114 cows, and 16 sheep and began its slow ride westward toward Nowa Sól, about 540 kilometers away. Like others before it, the train would advance a few stations at a time before coming to a standstill, waiting, and repeating the process all over again. Melania's head grew heavy that first day and night. Unable to fight off the drowsiness, she drifted in and out of sleep, losing count of all the times the train stopped and started. *Could one of the cows fall over from the train's rocking motion and crush somebody, and did she hear some Polish officers say that they couldn't advance because other trains were occupying the tracks*, she wondered, half asleep. She was indifferent to the miles of train tracks passing underneath, flashing through the cracks of the boxcar floor.

Days passed, and every evening the Polish soldiers would serve soup and black coffee to the adults as well as a roll to each child, which supplemented the bread, pork, and other provisions that Melania and her family had brought. The hardest part was collecting enough food for the farm animals. The Polish soldiers would provide some hay, but the passengers needed to search for more grass and water for their livestock whenever the train stopped during the daytime. At night, the Polish army would not allow the passengers to get out of their boxcars and locked everyone inside so that they could not escape.

Feces were another problem. The farm animals, defecating and urinating throughout the trip, created a nauseating smell. For sanitary reasons, the passengers were allowed to shovel the excrement out of the opened boxcar door while the train moved but not while it stood at the stations. Nevertheless, during the hot, summer days, the stench never really went away. To prevent the passengers from getting fleas, Polish soldiers walked through the boxcars spraying everyone and everything with an insecticide pump. Melania, still breastfeeding Julia, was exempt from being sprayed.

As they rode west, Melania would pour water into their wooden basin for Nadia, since the toddler would not stop moving and writhing about. Splashing and playing in the water kept her occupied as well as clean. Nobody else had such a chance to bathe.

The train stopped at the station in Oświęcim, where there were connections to both western and northern Poland, and transports were sent in different directions. The Polish soldiers ordered the passengers to get out of their boxcars and go into a building to get a shot that inoculated them against diseases like typhus. Melania, again, was excused.

Some passengers entered the building but never returned to their boxcars. Talk spread that the authorities were interrogating and arresting them for working with the Ukrainian nationalists. Some people said that they even heard screaming. In Oświęcim the authorities also arrested two men from Smerekowiec who were riding on other trains, Antoni Pawczyk and Piotr Dziamba, after someone denounced them as sympathizers of the Ukrainian Insurgent Army. Piotr Dziamba's poor wife ran around crying and desperately looking for her husband before having to depart without him, Melania heard.

The train continued westward to the industrial town of Katowice. Melania, sleeping, felt someone shake her. How could she sleep so much, her mother asked her, telling her that she needed to get up, look outside, and see how people in other places lived. Melania, annoyed at being awoken, raised her head to see factories, a sky gray with pollution, and the faint red circle of the sun outside the opened boxcar door. She told her mother that if it made her happy to look, then she should look. Melania then laid her head back down on the mattress.

Later during the journey, Dmytro wanted to clean the large cage that held their chickens, but when he opened the cage door, one of the chickens flew out, straight out the opened boxcar door. The chicken, a pretty white creature, landed in a field of grain. There was no way to retrieve her as the train moved onward.

The train pulled into the station in western Poland, in the town of Nowa Sól, during the first day or two of July. Not having enough power to make it up a hill a few kilometers before Nowa Sól, the train needed to wait for another locomotive to push it and finally arrived late in the evening. The Polish soldiers warned everyone that they could not leave their boxcars until the next morning and that anyone who disobeyed would be shot.

The following day, Melania and her family awoke and were told to pull their belongings off the train. The men went to reassemble their wagons and found that wagon parts had been stolen from the uncovered boxcars during the trip. Some people were missing one of their wheels, while Dmytro was missing the ladder on his wagon. Nevertheless, he and Seman began hitching a horse to each of their wagons and loading their things inside, while Wasyl took the cows and goat out to graze. As Wasyl walked off, Melania could hear him singing the Russian lyrics to the Soviet military song "Katyusha," which had been popular during the war: "*Vykhodila na bierieg Katiusha, na vysokii bierieg na krutoi.* Katyusha walked out onto the river bank, onto the high and steep bank." The animals, having consumed mostly dry hay during the trip, were devouring the green grass, tearing it out along with its roots. Maria and Hania, in the meantime, went off to explore a wild field near the station and brought back handfuls of berries—big, beautiful berries of a type that Melania had never seen growing in the Lemko region. After days of eating just the family's provisions, she savored their sweet taste.

Melania paced around outside the train station, with its crumbling sidewalks that looked as if the war had passed through yesterday instead of two years earlier. While keeping an eye on Nadia, she rocked and bounced baby Julia, who had started to cry as soon as they disembarked from the train and would not stop. Nothing Melania did to try to calm

The relocation of the Ukrainian population during Operation Vistula

down Julia, no amount of rocking, or shushing, or nursing, would make the baby stop screaming and choking on her own cries. Melania began to worry that something was wrong with her breast milk and that it had made Julia sick. She worried that the insecticide the Polish soldiers had sprayed had affected her after all.

Seman and Dmytro were told to report to the State Repatriation Office, or Państwowy Urząd Repatriacyjny, known as PUR. The State Repatriation Office informed them that they were being assigned to live in a village called Troska, about twenty kilometers away in the Zielona Góra district.

Melania and her family cleaned the boxcar of all the waste one last time. As they were finishing, though, a Polish soldier told Dmytro that they should not have bothered, because the Polish army was going to send the trains elsewhere to be washed and disinfected. Perhaps annoyed at doing work for nothing or perhaps because he had nowhere else to go, Dmytro climbed back into the boxcar, went over to a corner where a small pile of hay remained, pulled down his pants, squatted, and defecated. If the Polish army did not care about the dirty boxcar, then he would leave them with one.

4

Prisoners in the Central Labor Camp in Jaworzno

The Polish army and secret police had clear orders to arrest any Ukrainian civilians whom they suspected of assisting the UPA. General Mossor's special operational group, GO Wisła, gave them detailed instructions to compile lists of any "hostile and uncertain elements" among the Ukrainians. All the Ukrainians on the lists were to be noted with the letter A if they had been identified by the Department of Security's secret police, B if by the army, or C if through other kinds of reports, like those given by informants among people being relocated. The Polish soldiers and secret police then began seizing the suspected civilians at gathering points where villagers were waiting to be loaded into boxcars. They pulled suspects making their way across the country off the trains during station stops, like at Oświęcim. They even took Ukrainians directly from their homes and local churches while their villages were preparing to relocate. As part of Operation Vistula, the Polish authorities detained anyone thought to be a Ukrainian nationalist sympathizer and transported that person to a concentration camp in the city of Jaworzno.

Dmytro had not yet been relocated from Smerekowiec when one of his distant relatives, his sister-in-law's uncle, Pawel Kapitula, was arrested at home in the neighboring village, Żdynia. It was Sunday, June 8, 1947, and thirty-five-year-old Pawel had asked one of his brothers-in-law to come over and help him slaughter a hefty, 150-kilogram pig. Other villages had already been evacuated, so the people of Żdynia knew that their turn would come soon, and Pawel wanted to take along the meat. He and his brother-in-law had killed the pig, hung it up, cut off its head, and cleaned out its intestines when a military truck pulled up to Pawel's house and a couple of Polish army soldiers got out.

"*O, dla partyzantów szykuje mięso,*" one of the soldiers said accusingly in Polish as they walked up to Pawel. "Oh, he's preparing meat for the partisans."

"*Nie, nie dla partyzantów. Zbieram się na Zachód.* No, not for the partisans. I'm preparing to go west," Pawel answered. He recounted how a plane had flown over Żdynia earlier, dropping leaflets that told villagers not to be scared about the upcoming relocation because the entire Ukrainian population was going, and they would all receive farmland in their new place of residence.

The soldiers entered and began to search Pawel's house. They looked through some loose photographs, lingering over the old Kennkarte that the Germans had issued Pawel as identification during the war. They found two thousand zlotys in cash, which they confiscated. One of the military men came across a notebook with some numbers written in it. He seemed to believe they were the serial numbers of some kind of weapon, alleged proof of partisan activity. Smirking, he turned and struck Pawel in the face, while Pawel swore that he did not know what the numbers meant.

The soldiers ordered Pawel's brother-in-law, a Pole, to go home and Pawel to get into the military truck without saying where they were taking him. They then drove through Żdynia, searching for and arresting other suspected villagers, all simple farmers. They drove past the church and arrested a man who lived by the brook, followed by a father and a son. They stopped on top of the hill to seize two more men and then by some haystacks to seize another two. The soldiers also rode up to the house where the family of Pawel's sister-in-law lived and took away her brother, Damian Howansky, as his wife, Fotyna, stood sobbing and his five-year-old son, Stefan, watched. As the military truck stood outside the house for some time, Pawel's mother, alarmed by the news of her son's arrest, ran over and found him, slipping five hundred zlotys into his hands.

The soldiers drove everyone who was detained to the adjacent village of Małastów, which was already evacuated, and directed them into the basement of an empty house to sleep for the night. One of the men realized that the basement was not locked, however, and suggested that they run away. No, that would not be possible, Pawel warned, because the area was filled with soldiers, who were watching them and would shoot them right away if they tried to escape.

The interrogations began the next morning. A hulking officer summoned Pawel and grilled him with questions like "Did you kill your pig for the partisans? When did you last help the UPA bands? When did you come back from the forest? What is your pseudonym?" Pawel did not even know what "pseudonym" meant at first. He repeated that he had not helped any partisans hiding in the woods and that he had just been following instructions to prepare for relocation.

The Polish officers released some of the detainees, like the father and son from Żdynia, but drove Pawel and the others farther north to Gorlice, to yet another house basement. There Pawel was searched, and the soldiers took away the five hundred zlotys that his mother had given him. The detainees could hardly fit in this basement. They had to squeeze in beneath the stairs because the cellar was filled with so many arrested men and women from other Lemko villages like Pętna, Śnietnica, and Ropica.

The interrogations continued. The officers brought the detainees upstairs into the house one by one and beat them, often until they bled or lost consciousness, in order to force answers out of them. Those who admitted to working with the UPA were immediately shuttled off to one of the military courts for trial. Some of the detainees screamed so loudly during the beatings that Pawel heard a young boy's voice shout outside: "*Co robicie z tymi ludzmi?* What are you doing with those people?"

After a few days in Gorlice, Pawel and about sixty other detainees were all transported to the city's train station. They were loaded onto a train, packed into two of its covered cattle cars. Their train traveled no more than eight or nine kilometers, though, before it stopped. There was a small window at the top of the cattle car, so Pawel hoisted up one of the boys to look out and describe what he saw. They were at the Zagórzany station, the boy said, where it looked like masses of people were waiting at a gathering point with their belongings to be relocated.

Their train continued on, riding for hours until it reached the Jaworzno Szczakowa station, about thirty kilometers north of Oświęcim.

Pawel and the detainees were ordered to get out of their cattle cars and to start walking. Guarded by Polish soldiers, the group walked approximately eight kilometers, exhausted but aware that if anyone slowed down or stopped from fatigue, they would be punished. Finally, they reached the main gate of a camp with electric barbed-wire fencing all around it where a sign read Centralny Obóz Pracy w Jaworznie (Central Labor Camp in Jaworzno). Up above, from one of the dozen camp watchtowers, equipped with machine guns and spotlights, Pawel heard a soldier call out to the group's guards.

"*Dawaj tych partyzantów tutaj!*" the soldier shouted in Polish. "Bring those partisans here!"

"*Taki jesteś mądry—idź do lasu i złap ich!*" one of the guards heckled back. "You're so smart—go to the woods and catch them!"

The Nazis had originally established the concentration camp in Jaworzno in 1943 as a satellite of the Auschwitz camp and named it the SS-Lager Dachsgrube. Inmates, including Jews, Poles, and Soviet prisoners of war, supplied forced labor, working in coal mines. Those who became unable to work risked being sent to the gas chambers at Auschwitz. Soviet soldiers liberated the Jaworzno camp at the beginning of 1945. However, the Polish Communist government decided to restore the site, naming it the Central Labor Camp. The Central Labor Camp was not designed to exterminate its inmates but to isolate, punish, and dehumanize perceived enemies of the nation, including German prisoners of war, Nazi collaborators, and people with ethnically German roots who lived in Poland, known as Volksdeutsche.

Then, when the Polish government agreed to carry out Operation Vistula, talk began of establishing concentration camps for those Ukrainians considered a threat to the state. This would not be the first time that such a camp was established; before World War II, from 1934 until 1939, Poland's prewar government imprisoned political opponents and subversives, including members of the Organization of Ukrainian Nationalists, in the Bereza Kartuska prison. The Central Labor Camp in Jaworzno was designated for this same purpose, and on April 24, 1947, General Mossor gave orders for the Polish army to begin mass arrests of suspected Ukrainian civilians. The first group of Ukrainian prisoners was transported to Jaworzno in early May, just a month before Pawel.

The guards led Pawel, his sister-in-law's brother Damian, and the other new prisoners inside the Central Labor Camp and ordered them to wait in lines to be registered. It was June 13, 1947. Some officials arrived, and Pawel watched as a camp secretary suddenly pounced on and started kicking one of the female detainees. An officer commanded the secretary to stop, saying that her job was to take notes, not to beat the prisoners.

Pawel did not know exactly what was written on the papers that the officials held—where he was listed as inmate number 1712 and Damian was listed as inmate number 1708—but he saw how they used documents to sort the prisoners. When the officials pulled aside four older men and informed them that they could leave, Pawel assumed that the papers did not list much evidence against them. The freed men had just better not say anything to anyone about where they had been, the officials warned.

The officials then divided the remaining men from the women and assigned everyone to their barracks, which were numbered 1 to 14. Ukrainian men inhabited five barracks. Ukrainian women, some with small children, inhabited two. Barbed wire separated the men's barracks from the women's. Pawel was assigned to barrack 10, as was Damian. The barracks were long and consisted of three rooms, with each room containing at least 150 inmates, by Pawel's count.

The inmates had to share bunk beds constructed from wooden boards, which were nailed together in such a way that gaps were left between them. Two people slept on each bed, so Pawel and his bedmate could only fit if they both slept on their side. When one of them turned over, the other was forced to turn over as well.

Everyone received a gray camp uniform to wear—pants for the men and skirts for the women. Pawel would hang his pants on the post of the bed, slipping them on whenever any of the Polish soldiers, hundreds of which watched over the prisoners, came by on patrol. With only an empty sack to sleep on, which should have been filled with hay to cushion the hard bed but was not, Pawel used his overcoat as a pillow.

For the first weeks in Jaworzno, Pawel and the new inmates were interrogated individually every day. "What are the names of your father and mother? Where did you work? What sort of schooling did you have?" the officers asked. "When did you come back from the forest? What was your pseudonym? How many Poles did you kill?" the Polish officers would repeat over and over again. Pawel told them that he was innocent and that he had not done anything wrong, but the officers still ordered him to lie on the ground and struck him across the body and head with a rubber baton.

Pawel always made sure to answer the interrogation questions the same way each time, never offering more than necessary. He knew of people who had broken down during beatings, divulging whatever little information they knew about other inmates, in the hope that the Central Labor Camp officials would beat them less. But the officials just beat them more—often on the heels, causing more pain when they walked—in order to get more information out of them. They then tortured the other accused inmates too. The camp officials pressured prisoners, particularly those who admitted to being in the Ukrainian insurgency, into cooperating with them and telling on others.

Polish military intelligence knew that small groups of the UPA were continuing to fight in southeastern Poland, including in the woods of the Lemko region, but that they were greatly weakened. The Polish army's instructions were to do everything necessary to liquidate these groups quickly and completely. Army officials issued a secret order on July 19, 1947, that any relocated Ukrainians who illegally returned to their former places of residence—whether to gather their former crops or to form new UPA bands—were to be arrested and taken to the Department of Security, which would send them to the Central Labor Camp at Jaworzno. Polish officials from the Ministry of National Defense had also issued orders that those Ukrainians sent to the military court and given the death penalty for their activity in the UPA be executed on the same day.

Someone had also falsely informed on Pawel, he was sure. One of the other inmates from Żdynia, Seman Padła, told Pawel that, during an interrogation, he happened to see a signature on a document denouncing some of the people from their village. Seman recognized the signature immediately as that of his close friend. The friend had hidden in Seman's house after being resettled with his family from Żdynia to Soviet Ukraine and managing to escape back to the Lemko region using forged Polish birth certificates. His friend probably signed a document denouncing the villagers from Żdynia so that he would not be punished, Seman said.

Someone had to have falsely informed on him, Pawel was sure, because he had never worked with the UPA. He had heard of people from other villages who were members of the UPA, but he had never known UPA soldiers to come through Żdynia for longer than an hour or so, just long enough to take some bread or other food from the villagers' houses. Żdynia was too close to the border with Czechoslovakia, where border guards patrolled, for the UPA to have been very active there, the locals knew.

The demoralization of the Ukrainian prisoners, both male and female, was constant. The guards would order the men to run around their barracks and beat older inmates who lagged behind, breathing heavily as they struggled to keep up with the younger prisoners. The guards would conduct roll calls in the rain and make everyone stand in line for hours before allowing them to fall out and return to their barracks. The guards would also come into the women's barracks at night, tell them to line up their shoes, and then haphazardly throw the shoes outside, ordering the women to go find the ones that belonged to them.

For any reason at all, the guards would force the Ukrainian prisoners to do *zhabky*, or frog-jumps, squatting and hopping across the camp. The prisoners received a metal bowl from which to eat, and if they allowed even the slightest bit of rust to form on it, for example, they would have to do frog-jumps as punishment. So people started scrubbing their bowls with sand at the first sign of any rust to get rid of it.

The prisoners had no opportunity to properly wash themselves or their clothes and underwear, filthy from constant wear. Yet dirty feet were cause enough for a camp guard to punish an inmate. Lice, fleas, and bedbugs were common in the barracks. Scabies and typhus spread.

Many prisoners endured solitary confinement. Others heard threats that they would be sent to a camp in Siberia next. Some went insane from the physical and mental torment. One woman even threw herself against the electric fence after losing her mind. The camp authorities tossed all the bodies of the dead into an unmarked grave in the forest.

The prisoners received so little food—usually a sliver of bread, weak coffee, and some thin soup with maybe a tin can's worth of preserved meat minced into every fifty or one hundred liters—that they always went back to their barracks hungry. Starved, Pawel once snuck away some raw potatoes growing in the camp that the prisoners were forced to dig up. The potatoes were small enough that he was able to pop them, whole and unwashed, into his mouth. His stomach revolted because of the uncooked food, though, and he suffered with diarrhea for at least three days afterward. He took the advice of one of the men in his barrack not to eat anything except his daily ration of bread, dried out in the sun, until it passed.

Inmates who agreed to carry out beatings for the Polish officials received more food. The camp officials gave these inmates the status of *salowy*, the orderly in charge of a room in the barrack, or *barakowy*, the orderly in charge of the entire barrack, and were content to let the Ukrainian prisoners abuse one another. For some soup with extra fat on top, these inmates agreed to hurt their own people.

Pawel and a lot of the other male prisoners tried to stay away from one of the orderlies who was known to be crueler, a man by the name of Węgrzyn. He was a *fest khlop*—a big boy, as Pawel and other Lemkos said—who was built like a bull. Pawel and another inmate ran into Węgrzyn one time on the way to the latrine. Inmates were not allowed to go alone to the latrine—a large outhouse consisting of twelve holes in the ground across from another twelve holes in the ground—and always had to walk there in pairs, at minimum.

"Oh, I know you!" Węgrzyn said to Pawel when he saw him. "I know you from the partisan army!"

"I wasn't in the partisan army," Pawel answered with a serious tone, not wanting Węgrzyn to start spreading lies.

"Listen, do you have anything to smoke?" Węgrzyn then asked him. "Maybe you brought something with you?"

Pawel, who was wearing his overcoat, responded that, back in Żdynia, he had smoked a lot and always carried tobacco on him. He was even carrying some in his overcoat when he arrived at the camp, but the officials took everything from him. He checked his pockets, though, and wound up finding one leftover leaf. He gave it to Węgrzyn, who, maybe because of this gesture, never harmed Pawel afterward.

Pawel and the Ukrainian inmates were often required to do physical labor. Some of the men shoveled sand and hauled it in wheelbarrows to an area where other men dumped it out and used it to even out the ground. Still other men laid bricks and reconstructed buildings or walls, like a wall about sixty meters long and five meters tall that a huge thunderstorm destroyed as it passed through, tearing down electrical wires in Jaworzno in the process. The storm was retribution for punishing innocent people, everyone gossiped. Female inmates were given unprocessed wool, which they carded and spun into yarn; they knitted sweaters for the camp guards as the weather got cooler. The prisoners worked as cobblers and tailors, making shoes for the Polish army and shirts for the inmates in the various industrial workshops in the Central Labor Camp.

More than two dozen priests, mostly Greek Catholic but some Orthodox, were also imprisoned in the Jaworzno concentration camp. Ukrainian clergymen, like Ukrainian intelligentsia, were common among the inmates because of the simple fact that they taught religion or other subjects in the Ukrainian language, which often led to accusations of "spreading Ukrainian nationalist and enemy propaganda" followed by arrest and incarceration in the Central Labor Camp.

Among the imprisoned was Father Stefan Dziubyna, a Greek Catholic priest from the Lemko region who had a strong Ukrainian identity and had served the parish in Żdynia for a year before World War II. Months before the leaders of the Second Polish Republic fled and the Polish Communists eventually took over, the local government in charge of the Kraków Province had forced Father Dziubyna to leave Żdynia because of accusations that he was distributing Ukrainian propaganda and supporting the Ukrainian nationalists by giving the village children Ukrainian prayer books. Then, during the summer of 1947, when Father Dziubyna went to the gathering point at the Zagórzany train station to look for his family, who were waiting to be resettled, secret police from the Department of Security detained him. They took him to Jaworzno on June 15, only a few days after Pawel.

At first, Father Dziubyna was housed in Pawel's barrack. None of the inmates in the Central Labor Camp had books, but Father Dziubyna had managed to hold onto his prayer book somehow, so Pawel asked him if he could borrow it. Father Dziubyna showed Pawel which prayers in the book were only for priests and which ones he could use. Sometime later, however, the camp officials moved all the clergymen together into one barrack—barrack 12. The officials wanted to isolate the priests so that they would not be able to influence the other prisoners easily, Pawel guessed.

Pawel was sitting in barrack 12 one day, though, when an inmate did something to anger the orderly in charge. Pawel had no idea what exactly had happened to displease the orderly, but he knew that anything, really, could lead to a beating. The guards had once beaten Pawel just because he was wearing his overcoat on top of his uniform jacket, injuring him so badly that he could not sit normally on a chair for a while afterward and instead had to sit on his leg in a way that kept the injured bones from touching the seat. The angered orderly in barrack 12, a man by the name of Iwanow—who had a particular hatred for the clergy, many of the priests thought—picked up a wooden board. He tried handing it to one of the priests, commanding him to hit the offending inmate with it, but the priest refused. So Iwanow started hitting the priest with the board instead, and by the next day, the clergyman's entire backside was colored black with bruises.

Housed in separate barracks in the Central Labor Camp numbered 1 through 7 were German prisoners of war and a few Volksdeutsche, individuals with ethnic German roots who had been imprisoned at the end of the war. They were housed in the same camp and forced to work in the same mines where the Nazis, just a few years earlier, had sent their Jewish, Polish, and Soviet victims. Hauling sand one day, Pawel passed an older Volksdeutsche woman sitting next to her barrack window and singing to herself. Despite the fact that her son was serving in the Polish army, she was in the camp simply because she was a Volksdeutsche, she told Pawel.

Many Ukrainian inmates felt that the Germans in the Central Labor Camp were treated better. This was likely the case for the German prisoners of war because they were protected by the Geneva Convention's standards of international law concerning the humanitarian treatment of war victims. The Germans seemed to live in cleaner barracks and eat better food. They played musical instruments and sang. They had a separate hospital in the camp where German doctors and nurses who were also prisoners of war took care of the sick. Some fortunate Ukrainian inmates who were trained as physicians and pharmacists were eventually allowed to assist the German doctors, receiving extra servings of soup and fish oil at the hospital and escaping the violence of the camp.

Many months later, Pawel heard that Węgrzyn was made the orderly in one of the barracks where some German prisoners of war were held. Węgrzyn apparently walked into a room where two higher-ranking German officers were lying in their beds and ordered them to get up, but they did not listen to him. Treating them as he did his fellow Ukrainian inmates, he tried to punish them. However, the German officers would have none of Węgrzyn's abuse and beat him so badly that he landed in the hospital for a few weeks. Węgrzyn emerged from the hospital using crutches and was said never to beat another prisoner again.

With the colder fall weather came more deaths and the spread of disease. Inmates were swollen from hunger. A woman who was arrested while pregnant and whose exhausted body gave birth to an underweight baby boy while in the camp had to turn to stronger mothers to nurse him. A Lemko man from Pawel's neighboring village of Gładyszów wasted away from starvation. The man was larger than Pawel and might have stayed alive, but he despaired about ever leaving Jaworzno. Depressed, he had no appetite and would not eat. He was finally found unconscious and died shortly after.

Pawel was growing thin when he suddenly received a package from his wife, Maria—his first and only contact with his family. He had no idea how, but she managed to pass some clothing on to him. She gave him a pair of wooden clogs, replacing the shoes that Pawel had worn every day since his arrest. The shoes were falling apart despite the rubber soles from the cobbler's workshop that he had added to them. She also gave him a jacket and two sweaters, one of which he traded for another inmate's ration of bread and the second of which he wore as the days grew colder.

Other prisoners also began to receive packages. Perhaps the family members had learned that their loved ones were in Jaworzno from the Ukrainians who had been released, or perhaps they had paid somebody like a Polish official or lawyer to find them, or perhaps they had heard about Jaworzno because of the former inmates who were being tried in court, Pawel thought. Regardless, desperate family members showed up at the gates of the concentration camp, close enough to see prisoners working in the distance but only able to hand the packages over to the guards and hope to God that they would be delivered.

The camp officials considered the evidence against the inmates, determining which to send for trial and which to be released. For weeks, they took photographs of the inmates and made identification cards for all of them. Pawel, like the others in his barrack, had to sit down for the photo with a sign hanging on a string around his neck. His name and other personal information were written on the sign.

One cold evening, when the camp seemed emptier than it had been for months, with dozens of prisoners having been hauled off to court, Pawel got ready for bed. He had already climbed into an empty top bunk, where he thought it would be a little warmer, when the barrack and room orderlies came in to conduct a review. The orderlies latched onto one of the inmates, named Stefan Chrystyna, who had been sleeping near Pawel, and yelled at him for not having washed his feet sufficiently. Long ago, Pawel had learned to carry a piece of cloth with him before he went to sleep, into which he would spit or, in the worst case, urinate so that he could clean his feet. The orderlies pulled the inmate from his bed and hit him with wooden boards. They hit him hard, but he was tough and did not scream. Swearing at him, they then hit him harder with the edges of the boards. They broke so many of his bones that he died within a few days.

On January 5, 1948, with no notice, Polish officials released Pawel from the Central Work Camp. The officials just informed him that he was going home to his family, and that was it. They gave him an identification card—essentially a small, flimsy piece of paper on which his photo was glued and his name and date of birth were written. The card also stated in typed words that he had been discharged from arrest that day and was returning to his place of permanent residence. They gave him back the two thousand zlotys that the Polish soldiers had confiscated from his house almost seven months earlier, but not the five hundred that his mother had given him. They required all the inmates to sign a document agreeing to keep secret what they had seen and heard while in the camp or else face punishment.

Polish soldiers led Pawel and the other inmates released that day to the train station. Pawel left behind his old rubber-soled shoes and walked away from Jaworzno in the pair of wooden clogs that his wife had sent him. In the concentration camp, the Polish soldiers had required the prisoners to salute when walking past them or else risk punishment. Now, however, beyond the camp walls and in the free world, the soldiers forbid the former inmates from saluting them, as if they were embarrassed by the demand.

Pawel and the other Ukrainians boarded a train to the city of Poznań, more than four hundred kilometers westward. They would not be returning to southeastern Poland because their families no longer lived there. Pawel would find out later that Damian Howansky had been released too and had boarded a train to the western city of Wrocław to rejoin his family in the village of Dębno. He would also find out that some of the people released from Jaworzno killed one of the Ukrainian orderlies who had beaten up his own people at the camp, throwing him out of their boxcar on yet another train.

Pawel would be counted as one of 3,873 Ukrainians imprisoned in the Jaworzno concentration camp as part of Operation Vistula. Because of torture, starvation, disease, and suicide, approximately 160 of these inmates never made it out of the camp alive.

Pawel's train arrived in Poznań on January 6—the Feast of the Three Kings for the Poles but Christmas Eve for the Ukrainians, according to the Julian calendar. The Polish soldiers informed him that his new place of residence would be the village of Machary, which was in the county of Strzelce, a few hours farther away. Pawel and the other released inmates continued on by train and then by foot to Strzelce. As they walked, the Polish secret police surrounded them and led them to the basement of a house, ordering the owners to feed them. It was close to one o'clock in the morning by the time Pawel and the others ate cabbage soup that the owners prepared.

The next day, the Polish officials called for cars and horse-drawn wagons to transport the released prisoners to their assigned villages, places that they had never been to before with names like Brzoza, Sławno, and Bronowice. The horse-drawn wagon that was supposed to take Pawel did not come until evening. He and two other men climbed into it and rode about a dozen kilometers to the village of Bobrówko, where the families of both men now lived. The Polish officials dropped Pawel off along with the two men, telling him to go, even though his village, Machary, was still a kilometer or two away.

"*Ta de pidu?* But where will I go?" he thought. He did not know where his family had been relocated, and it was dark already.

The officials told Pawel just to keep walking, so he proceeded down the German-built cobblestone road. He walked and walked in the cold until he saw a light about 150 meters away from the road. Separating him from the light were some woods, which he decided not to cross in the dark. He continued a bit farther down the road, past a barn, and walked through some kind of park before realizing that the light was coming from the window of a house. Pawel walked up to the windowsill and immediately saw his wife and his sister-in-law moving around inside. It was Christmas night for the Ukrainians, and he was sure that God had led him to them. Pawel started crying while standing outside looking at his family. He knocked on the window. After a second or two, he heard one of the women, who saw his face in the light, call out, "*Pavlo priishov! Pawel has come!*"

5

A New Home in the Recovered Territories?

Standing outside the Nowa Sól train station that July 1947, waiting to be led to their new village, the Pyrtej family learned that any relocated Ukrainians who did not own a horse-drawn wagon would be driven in army trucks. The Polish officials assigned two trucks to drive to Troska, where less than a dozen families from Smerekowiec, including the Pyrtej family, were being relocated. Dmytro told Melania that because their baby, Julia, had not stopped crying since disembarking from the train, Melania should get into one of the trucks with all the children and women in their family so that they could ride to the village more quickly. Dmytro, Seman, and Wasyl would finish the trip in the family's wagons along with all their belongings and farm animals. Dmytro's parents and siblings would also ride in their wagons to Troska.

Melania climbed into the front seat of the first army truck with her two daughters. They sat right next to the Polish driver, who looked at colicky Julia with some concern. Maria and Hania climbed into the back of the vehicle. Also aboard the two trucks were other former inhabitants of Smerekowiec with all their baggage: Seman's widowed brother Danko, a man named Pawlo Pupczyk with his young daughter and elderly mother, and a blacksmith named Marko Astrab with his son and four nephews. Marko Astrab had agreed to watch over his nephews so that they would not have to walk the approximately twenty kilometers to Troska alongside their parents' packed wagon. The boys' father promised the four of them that he and their mother would arrive in Troska by wagon not long after they did and gave each son a bread roll to eat during the trip. The boys devoured their rolls before the trucks even pulled away from the train station.

The two trucks set out for Troska in the late afternoon. They rode slowly through villages and towns with brick buildings that had been inhabited by Germans just a few years earlier but now possessed Polish names, like Kożuchów instead of Freystadt in Schlesien and Mirocin Dolny instead of Nieder Herzogswaldau. They drove down tree-lined roads that were twice as wide as those in the Lemko region, remarking that it seemed as if the Germans had spared no land to build those roads. When the trucks passed some people working in the fields, Marko Astrab's son saw a boy taking cows out to pasture and recognized him as a former classmate who had been relocated earlier. He shouted the boy's name from the truck, but the classmate only managed to wave before the vehicles drove past him and he was out of sight. As they then rode through a village called Jarogniewice, Melania saw a woman outside wearing a traditional Lemko corset over her blouse and an apron over her pleated skirt. From the front seat, Melania turned and pointed out the woman to her mother, noting that she had to be from the Lemko region too.

Not far past Jarogniewice, the trucks turned onto a clay pathway bordered by overgrown brush. They approached a wooden bridge, which crossed the narrow section of a river, and the driver of the first truck stopped in front of it. Worried that the bridge, which was built for wagons, could not bear the weight of the army trucks, he refused to drive over it. He told all the passengers that they would have to get out and walk the last hundred meters to Troska, carrying whatever baggage they had.

Marko Astrab protested, though, declaring that if the bridge collapsed from the weight, then it collapsed, and so be it. He had lost everything already, so it did not matter much if he lost whatever was left, but he would not carry his many suitcases and sacks the rest of the way. He examined the bridge together with the driver, eventually convincing him to finish transporting all their belongings to Troska as long as the passengers, particularly the women and children, were not in the vehicles as they crossed the bridge.

Melania climbed out of the truck with her daughters and walked toward Troska with Julia now calmly lying in her arms and Nadia toddling by her side. As they entered the village on foot, the first thing that Melania saw were brick houses with smashed windows and no doors, as if someone had wanted to let the new inhabitants know that they were not welcome. She glanced around, expecting to see a village full of people, but the place was empty. All she heard was the chirping of a sole cuckoo bird. She had thought that villagers would be working in the fields, as they did in the Lemko region at this time of year. However, nothing was sown in the surrounding land, meaning that there would be nothing to eat come harvest time. The gardens were overgrown with weeds and nettles, and only a few peonies left to fend for themselves had survived. Melania felt the blood rush out of her face. *How are we going to live here? What are we going to do?* she thought.

The drivers parked the trucks near one of the houses with a big yard and instructed everyone to unload their baggage. Pawlo Pupczyk, who had worked in the local cooperative store back in Smerekowiec, begged one of the drivers to take them back to some town, any town. At least in a more populated area he might have a chance to find a job in some shop or factory. Trying to bargain, Pawlo promised to give the driver the American suits he owned just to take them somewhere else. But the driver refused, saying that his orders were to transport the group to Troska and that he would be punished if he transported them anywhere else. Strict orders about the distribution of Ukrainians in the so-called Recovered Territories, stipulating that the concentration of Ukrainian families in any district population could not exceed 10 percent, had come all the way from the top Polish officials in the Politburo of the Central Committee of the Polish Workers' Party. Following their orders to drop off their passengers in Troska, the drivers of the two army trucks simply drove away.

Melania had no idea how long it would take for Dmytro, Seman, Wasyl, or any of the other families traveling by wagon to arrive with their things. Only about an hour remained before sunset, and everyone in Troska was hungry and thirsty. There was no milk to drink, since all their cows were walking alongside the wagons, and whatever money anyone had to buy food was useless, since no store was to be found. They could have had bread to eat if they had known not to feed it all to the cows after they stepped off the train in Nowa Sól, Marko Astrab lamented. Luckily, Melania's uncle Danko had brought a crate of potatoes with him on the truck, so the group built a campfire and baked some. They ate hot potatoes along with some wild red berries that the children found and picked nearby.

By nightfall, none of the wagons had yet arrived. Discovering that the brick ovens in all the houses had been smashed just like the windows, the group decided to take shelter from the cool night air in one of the barns. They found some hay and spread it on the barn's brick floor. Pawlo Pupczyk then placed his only down blanket on top of the hay so that everyone would be able to lie at least on a bit of something soft. The adults hugged the children to try to keep them warm, and, with their heads all close together, the group—talking, crying, and laughing as much as they could—finally fell asleep.

When Melania woke up the next morning, the sun was shining and her mother was standing before her, offering her some milk. While Melania slept, Maria had walked back down the pathway they had driven on the day before to the house in Jarogniewice where they had seen the woman in Lemko dress. Maria found out that the woman had indeed been relocated from the Lemko village of Pętna with her two daughters a few weeks earlier, after her husband was arrested for cooperating with the UPA and taken away. Maria asked the woman if she might have any milk to spare for the children in Troska and brought back two liters in a metal pot that the woman loaned to her for everyone to share. Melania turned the shallow cover of the pot upside down and poured some milk from the pot into it so that she could take some sips.

Melania then went for a walk with Julia and Nadia around their new village in order to get a better look inside the houses; but with each destroyed home she entered, she felt worse. Not long after, Dmytro, Seman, Wasyl, and the rest of the families rode into Troska, led by Polish soldiers. Melania rushed over to Dmytro, sharing one thought after another: that Troska was a God-forsaken place; that she had looked at the houses but that most were damaged; that there was one house that she thought might be all right, but she wanted to show it to him; and that she was worried and did not know what they were going to do.

Calming her down, Dmytro said in Lemko, "*My damy sobi rady. Iakosy budeme zhyty.* We'll make do. Somehow we'll live."

Dmytro began unpacking their belongings so that they could wash up and cook something to eat. He, Seman, and Wasyl had spent the night with the other people in the wagons as well as the Polish soldiers who were guiding them in a field in a neighboring village, Dmytro explained to Melania. They had been only a few kilometers away but had not known that they were so close to Troska.

Melania and Maria pulled some potatoes out of one of their wagons, peeled them, and began preparing potato soup. They got water from a nearby well, heated it in a pot over a fire, and tossed in the potatoes along with some dried meat for flavor. Other people's meat had spoiled in the summer heat and had to be thrown away earlier in the trip, but the Pyrtejs still had some of their dried meat. The women also sliced bread and spread lard that was leftover from the train ride onto it. Finally, sitting outside on their unloaded wooden storage chests, the family ate their first meal all together in western Poland.

The house that Melania chose was the third one or so from the main pathway to the village. She picked it without any arguments from the rest of her family or from the other people assigned to Troska. There was no point in fighting about houses, they all felt, when nobody was even sure whether they would stay in western Poland for very long or whether the rumors were true that the Polish government would allow them to go back to the Lemko region shortly.

The house was smaller than many of the others in Troska, with only two rooms and a kitchen that together were not as spacious as the one big room that the family had shared back in Smerekowiec. Melania liked it, though, because it was constructed from red brick instead of wood and looked solid, with strong walls. She, Dmytro, and their girls could sleep in one room, while her parents, Hania, and Wasyl could sleep in the other.

Melania's only concern was that the German who had lived in the house before them—a tailor, they would later find out—never built a proper barn for horses. There was only a little stable where the family could keep their cows. This stable was nothing like the family's large barn with the wooden floor of which Maria had been so proud in the Lemko region.

The Pyrtej family also had to get rid of all the mosquitoes that infested the house. Melania had never seen so many mosquitoes before. Drawn to the nearby stagnant river, they had probably entered the house through its broken windows, the family figured. They seemed to cover every inch of every room, making the walls a darker shade than they actually were. Nobody could stand being inside for long because the mosquitoes would launch into the air at the slightest movement and attack, leaving swollen bumps all over everyone's faces and bodies.

On her second night in Troska, Melania slept with Dmytro and their children outside on a mattress, while the rest of her family slept near them on makeshift beds crafted from blankets and pillows atop fresh hay. The family members giggled when they saw one of their neighbors create a bed out of an abandoned armoire by laying it on its back and putting hay inside it. They teased him that he was sleeping inside a closet.

The following morning, to exterminate the mosquitoes, the family lit bunches of paper with matches and waved the torches around. They burned off the mosquitoes' wings and swept up their remains with a broom. Melania just prayed that they would not burn down the entire house in the process.

Dmytro grabbed his hammer and nailed bed sheets over the broken windows as well as a heavy woolen blanket over the missing door. The family also swept up the pieces of the smashed brick oven, which had left the house smelling of ash. Melania and Maria carried out dozens of basketfuls of broken bricks so that Dmytro could start rebuilding a new oven soon. By the end of the day, the Pyrtej family were able to move into their new house.

Some of the people sent to Troska left within the first few days, like Marko Astrab and Pawlo Pupczyk. They heard about a state-run collective farm in the nearby village of Kożuchów and pleaded with the head of the farm to let them work for him, so he arranged for them to move there. The Pyrtej family, hearing talk about how other Lemkos had fled back to their homes in southeastern Poland and been jailed for returning illegally, decided to stayed where they had been assigned, however.

The Feast of Saint John, called Ivan Kupalo Day by the Ukrainians, came and went without any commemoration during that first week in Troska. Usually in Smerekowiec the villagers would mark Ivan Kupalo Day, the holiday of the summer solstice, by decorating the rooms of their houses with leafy branches so that everything was covered in green. Exhausted from the trip and separated from their former community, though, the Pyrtej family did not celebrate the tradition.

Before long, Poles living in neighboring villages made their way down the pathway to Troska. These Poles had arrived in the Recovered Territories a few years earlier, having been expelled from Poland's former eastern territories during the Soviet-Polish population exchange of 1944 to 1946. Because they had arrived immediately after the former German inhabitants evacuated, many spoke of how the Germans had left behind paintings on the walls, bread in the ovens, and cattle tied up in barns. Melania heard her family and friends refer to these Poles as *repatrianci zza Buga*, repatriates from beyond the Bug River. They had migrated from areas like Wołyń, now Volhynia in Soviet Ukraine, where conflict between the Polish and Ukrainian populations had been violent and where Ukrainian nationalists during World War II had been accused of wishing to remove all Poles from Ukrainian lands in their fight to create an independent Ukrainian nation-state. Poles from Wołyń had reported massacres of men, women, and children in their villages, with Ukrainian partisans burning their homes, shooting those who tried to flee, and killing others with axes and pitchforks.

Fearing the Ukrainian nationalists, many Poles from beyond the Bug River had worried that all the Ukrainians relocated to the Recovered Territories were *banderowcy*, or Banderites, supporters of the OUN leader Stepan Bandera. Feeling threatened, these Poles had been the ones to smash all the windows and ovens in Troska, the Pyrtej family eventually found out. For protection, they had slept with axes underneath their pillows when the transports of Ukrainians had first arrived in western Poland. They had gone to bed each night with weapons until they realized that they were not in any danger.

The Polish neighbors now came to Troska offering villagers the opportunity to work for them. The men could dig potatoes and the young women could take cows out to pasture in exchange for grain so that they would not starve to death. Seman once went to harvest rye for a Polish family but then decided that the fifteen kilograms of grain he earned were not worth the long day in someone else's field.

Seman and Dmytro went to search for jobs elsewhere and, within weeks, learned about a sawmill looking for workers about thirty kilometers away from Troska. The Germans had previously run the sawmill, but now it belonged to the Polish government. Having spent their entire lives working in the forests around Smerekowiec, Seman, Dmytro, and a few more people from Troska who owned horse-drawn wagons began to cut and haul lumber for the sawmill. They would chop trees from the thick forests that the Germans had planted near Troska, deliver the lumber to the sawmill, and then stop off to buy potatoes and grain by the wagon-load in towns like Kożuchów, where the land was more fertile. With the money made from hauling, the family no longer had to worry about what they would eat until they could harvest their own crops.

Melania bought a pair of twin beds on the cheap from one of the Polish women who had come from beyond the Bug River and had first access to the furniture the Germans left behind. The beds were used and dirty, but Melania cleaned them. She slept on one of the beds and Dmytro slept on the other, giving up their hay-filled mattress and big bed frame to Maria, Seman, and Hania to share. Wasyl, meanwhile, slept on an old couch. Maria found yet another small bed in one of the empty German houses. Dmytro added rockers to the bottom of it, creating a big cradle that Julia and Nadia could be rocked in at the same time. Little Nadia liked to sing songs that Dmytro had taught her as she rocked.

From one of the abandoned houses nearby, Dmytro also took some glass to fix their house's windows as well as a real front door. From the wood that he cut and hauled to the sawmill, he rebuilt the ladder that had been stolen from his wagon on the train ride to western Poland and constructed a barn with Seman in which to house the family's horses. From some white-colored bricks that the Germans had left behind in piles in Troska—as if they had planned to build something with them before being evacuated—Dmytro created a sidewalk in front of the house so that the family would not have to walk in the mud when it rained.

One Sunday a few weeks after arriving in Troska, Melania welcomed a visitor. Her former neighbor from Smerekowiec, Stefania Smereczniak, whose husband, Andriy, had been the first to alert Melania to the Ukrainians being relocated from Gorlice and whom Melania had not seen since they were all forced to leave their village, showed up on her doorstep. Stefania had walked more than fifteen kilometers from the city of Zielona Góra to Troska on her way to find her family in a nearby village.

Melania cried when she saw her friend. Right away, she gave her water to wash her feet, since Stefania had been walking barefoot, with her shoes in her hands, like they always had in the Lemko region. They would walk to church or elsewhere barefoot and then clean their feet and put their shoes on at the last minute to try to preserve them. Melania and Stefania only had a short time to sit down and talk, exchanging news about who lived where now and how they were doing, before Stefania had to be back on her way.

Old friends relocated to villages not too far away began to come to Troska in search of relatives, but after their visits, plainclothes detectives would often follow them. The local Polish authorities monitored the Ukrainian population, inquiring who visitors were and why they had come. The detectives even paid off local villagers, usually with better housing, to spy and inform on their neighbors, Melania heard. Whenever the detectives approached her with any questions, Melania answered that she did not know anything.

Slowly, the Pyrtej family began to piece together information about their friends and family scattered throughout the area and to try to rebuild their community. Maria found her mother and visited her in Milicz, although Melania never had a chance to see her grandmother again in the years before she passed away. By the time the last transport of Ukrainians arrived in the Recovered Territories in mid-August 1947, the Polish government had relocated and dispersed more than ten thousand people, along with the Pyrtej family, throughout the Zielona Góra Province. In a little over three months, from April 29 to August 12, the government removed between 140,000 and 150,000 Ukrainians from the Kraków, Rzeszów, and Lublin Provinces by the southeastern border of Poland and relocated them across the country through Operation Vistula.

After months passed in Troska with no news from the Polish authorities about permission to return to southeastern Poland, the Pyrtej family realized that they would not be going back to the Lemko region soon. Their only contact with the government was when they collected corn feed for their farm animals, which the relocated Ukrainians could obtain from the local municipality every month or so based on the number of people in their household. The Pyrtej family fed the corn feed to a pig they bought, growing it big and fat. Melania regretted that her family had sold their newborn calf back at the train station in Zagórzany, thinking that she could have raised it in the Recovered Territories after all.

In the fall, as Hania started the school year at the local Polish elementary school in Jarogniewice, her family planted their first crops, some rye. They bought fertilizer and spread it over the half-dozen hectares of land that the local municipality had apportioned to them in Troska, which was poor quality and sandy and less than what they had left behind in the Lemko region. At the same time, the Polish government carried out plans to take control of the Ukrainian population's former land in the southeast, decreeing on September 5, 1947, that any movable or immovable property left in Poland by those who were resettled in the Soviet Union, including Petro and his in-laws, became property of the state upon the moment of resettlement, without any compensation.

In the winter, when the holidays arrived, the Pyrtej family sang Ukrainian carols, like "Nova Radist' Stala" and "Boh Predvichnyi," in their home; but as Greek Catholics, they had no church of their own. On December 24 the family traveled to the Roman Catholic Church in the nearby village of Broniszów to celebrate Pasterka, midnight mass, with the Poles. Melania, now pregnant with her third child, stayed home to watch over her sleeping daughters. She missed the ease of walking to the Greek Catholic church in Smerekowiec and chatting with her neighbors after the service, delivered in Church Slavonic rather than Latin like the Polish mass. Thirteen days later, the family celebrated the Ukrainian holiday of Christmas Eve as they always had, following the Julian calendar. They prepared food such as oat soup, pierogies with prunes, and potatoes with mushroom sauce—twelve dishes without any meat or milk, the traditional Ukrainian Christmas Eve holy supper representing Jesus Christ's last meal with the twelve apostles.

At the beginning of 1948, the Pyrtej family began to learn of the release of prisoners from the Jaworzno concentration camp. The men from Smerekowiec who had been arrested at the Oświęcim station appeared in their families' villages, as did the husband of the Lemko woman in Jarogniewice who had given milk to Maria when she first came to western Poland. Repaying the woman's kindness, Maria brought her and her husband some salted pork from the Pyrtej family's recently slaughtered pig.

A letter from Petro arrived all of a sudden one day. From the return address on the envelope, the family found out that he was living in the city of Stanisławów in western Soviet Ukraine and not somewhere farther east, where he had been headed the last they had heard from him. He wrote that he had tried to contact them in Smerekowiec but that his letters always returned, marked undeliverable. Finally, through relatives who were also resettled to Soviet Ukraine and who had contact with the Pyrtej family, he learned that they had been relocated to western Poland. After more than two years of no communication with Petro, two years of worrying about him, the Pyrtej family read that he and Olya were healthy and that Petro was grateful to know that everyone was alive.

Through subsequent letters mailed between Soviet Ukraine and western Poland, the Pyrtej family learned that Petro and Olya had welcomed their first child, a baby girl named Myroslava, in May 1948, and Petro learned that Melania and Dmytro had welcomed their first son, whom they also named Petro, a few months later, in September. When Melania went into labor with her son, Dmytro was home, taking a break from sowing rye in their fields. They did not know of any midwives in western Poland, so Dmytro drove Melania by wagon to the hospital in Kożuchów. Melania could not help but worry that people would gossip about how she went to the hospital instead of giving birth at home, as they had always done in Smerekowiec.

Separated from their old community and channels of information, Melania's family did not hear much outside news in Troska. They heard nothing about the trial that summer in Warsaw of the Ukrainian Insurgent Army members charged with assassinating General Świerczewski. President Bolesław Bierut refused to grant any pardon to the accused, and so nine UPA soldiers from the Stakh, Khrin, Krylach, and Bir divisions were sentenced to death and executed on August 28, 1948, while another twelve received long prison terms. The Polish government had achieved victory over the Ukrainian insurgents. Now that Operation Vistula had cleared the Ukrainian population out of southeastern Poland, the UPA's leadership was ordering most of its squadrons there to demobilize and leave.

Smyrnyi, Olya's old friend from the Ukrainian teachers' seminary, also received orders to try to make his way to the American zone of occupation in Germany. At first, he was told to remain with just a group of his best members; but they had no local population to help them, and the Polish military forces, realizing the weakness of Smyrnyi's group, kept boldly attacking the forests. After months of difficulty, Smyrnyi and his group finally escaped on foot through Czechoslovakia and then Austria until they crossed the border into Germany and surrendered their weapons to the American military command in the municipality of Obernzell on September 29, 1948. Risking arrest, Smyrnyi would make his way from Germany to Poland and back to Germany once more the following year, this last time with his fiancée and future wife, Maria Bajus. Maria had been imprisoned for assisting the UPA, sent to the Jaworzno concentration camp as inmate number 2313, sentenced to ten years in jail, and only released after her father spent on a Polish lawyer the dollars he had earned working in America. The couple would eventually immigrate to Canada.

Melania's family likewise heard little about the political situation within Poland. They were not aware of the growing struggle among the Communists in Poland, as hard-line supporters of Stalin, like Bolesław Bierut, who became the first secretary general of the ruling Polish United Workers' Party by the end of 1948, faced resistance from those who disagreed with the Soviet Union's continued involvement in Polish internal affairs, like Władysław Gomułka. They were also not aware when, the following year, on July 27, 1949, the Polish leadership issued another decree stating that the government could also now take possession of any property that owners no longer occupied in the southeastern provinces of Poland, meaning that Seman no longer had any legal claim to his home in the Lemko region. Some relocated Ukrainians had managed to escape unlawfully back to their former villages. But many others tried the legal route, sending petitions and letters to government bodies asking that they be allowed to move back, only to receive responses that return was not possible because their properties were now under new ownership.

Melania had no time to pay attention to politics, like Poland's transition to a centrally planned socialist economy, or its nationalization of private industry, or its attempt to collectivize agriculture in line with the Soviet model. She would have no idea that, during their struggle for power, the Polish government's hard-line Stalinists would eventually turn against and issue long-term sentences to military leaders such as Stefan Mossor and Michał Żymierski in a show trial in the summer of 1951, or that they would use the Central Labor Camp in Jaworzno next as a facility to incarcerate young Poles who were arrested while taking part in political opposition movements. She focused on taking care of her family and raising her children, giving birth to yet another son, named Stefan, in the hospital in the early 1950s. Her daughter Nadia was now old enough to go to Polish school in Jarogniewice, walking with one of her older cousins through forests and fields all the way from Troska and back, often resting under a pine tree in the middle of the two-kilometer route.

Hania was already in her first year of middle school when she got sick. She was living in a dormitory in the town of Szprotawa, more than thirty-five kilometers away from Troska, when she at first thought that she had some sort of stomach virus. After three or four days of lying in bed, though, she could not move. Completely paralyzed, she was rushed to a hospital in the city of Poznań and diagnosed with widespread inflammation of the nerves. She underwent about four months of treatment in the hospital before the doctors released her, sending her back to Troska and then to a sanatorium, a medical facility for long-term illnesses, in the town of Iwonicz-Zdrój. Iwonicz-Zdrój sat in a valley of the low, rolling Carpathian Mountains, where patients could recuperate while taking in the clean air and local mineral waters. Because of her illness, Hania was the first person in her family to be able to visit southeastern Poland again.

Following her stay in the sanatorium, Hania traveled from Iwonicz-Zdrój to Smerekowiec, only a short distance away. She slept at the house of an old family friend, a Lemko woman who, like others, had been able to remain because she was married to a Pole. The woman accompanied Hania to visit the old Pyrtej house, where a *góralka*—a female from one of the native groups of highlanders of southern Poland—was now living. The Polish authorities had encouraged the poorer highlanders to occupy many of the homes left behind by the relocated Lemkos. The *góralka* hosted Hania kindly with some *rosiv* and *komperi*, as the Lemkos in Smerekowiec called chicken broth and potatoes. Hania ate inside the big main room that the Pyrtej family had once shared where her family's table and benches still stood. For the next three or four days, Hania stayed in Smerekowiec. She visited the church where she had been christened and even danced and drank with the highlanders at one of their celebrations before traveling back to Troska and telling her parents all that she had seen in their old village. Within a year, though, the Pyrtej family received news that the *góralka* had accidentally burned down their old house when something supposedly went awry and caught on fire while she was making moonshine.

Local government offices in the Recovered Territories were not giving the relocated Ukrainians enough help, the Central Committee of the Polish United Workers' Party admitted in a secret resolution that was made public in April 1952, just months before Poland officially changed its name to the People's Republic of Poland. The resolution acknowledged that Ukrainians spoke their language at home but Polish in public out of a fear of being persecuted and that many, particularly those who were Greek Catholic, could not practice their faith and celebrate their holidays openly—just as the Pyrtej family had experienced. It also acknowledged that local governments continued to see the Ukrainians as enemies, which is why those governments allowed political and cultural discrimination against the Ukrainians. As a result, about three thousand of the relocated Ukrainians had already escaped from the Recovered Territories and returned to their former homes. Immediate changes needed to be made to the situation of the Ukrainians, normalizing their economic conditions and permitting their cultural needs, in order to prevent further illegal returns, the Central Committee of the Polish United Workers' Party stated.

The house that Melania had chosen in Troska ultimately became too crowded for both Melania's father and her husband. Seman and Dmytro argued often—about money and about how to run their farm. When they got paid for hauling wood together, Dmytro protested to Melania that Seman took control of the money, not even giving him enough to buy a package of cigarettes. As head of the household, Seman seemingly felt that he was in charge of everything they owned. He had never really approved of his son-in-law, despite the fact that he always praised him to other people, saying that nobody could put a horseshoe on a horse like Dmytro and that Dmytro could do anything.

Tired of the fighting, Dmytro warned Seman that he would leave along with his wife and children. "*Nianiu, ia povim zhe ia vas lyshu. Ia pidu desy inde zhyty.* Father, I'm telling you that I'll leave you. I'll go somewhere else to live," Melania heard Dmytro tell Seman in Lemko.

"*To ydy. Ia tia ne trymam. Ale lem sy toto ber shcho z prynius.* So go. I'm not holding you back. But only take what you brought with you," Seman responded, rubbing in the fact that Dmytro had come to their household with practically nothing.

The next day, Dmytro went to Jarogniewice, to the local Państwowe Gospodarstwo Rolne, or PGR, as the state-run collective farms were now called, and found a job repairing wagons. There were no empty houses on the territory of the PGR, but he could work there until one became available, he was told. Melania thought that her father was not being fair to Dmytro, but she cried at the idea of leaving her family after they had all lived together for so long. She did not want to move and wondered how she would cope in Jarogniewice.

"*Khochesh ostaty, to ostan'. Ia pidu sam.* If you want to stay, then stay. I'll go by myself," Dmytro told her. He was working at the PGR every day and just sleeping in Troska at night. Melania would cook dinner, but Dmytro would always come home late to eat because he refused to sit alongside Seman.

Finally, after a few months, around March 1953, the PGR informed Dmytro that it had a house for him. Melania agreed to leave, respecting her husband's wishes. She and Dmytro packed their children and the few items that they owned, including the two beds Melania had bought from the Polish woman beyond the Bug River, before departing for Jarogniewice. Their new house—the first where they lived on their own—had big windows in front and a number of rooms for their family to grow.

That same March, the loudspeakers at the PGR, which could be heard from every worker's house, broadcast the news that Joseph Stalin had died. Everyone talked about how life would change following the Soviet leader's death. Melania, however, did not believe that to be true—there had been and would still be Communists in power.

Melania was home in Jarogniewice during the following winter of 1954, taking care of her fifth child, a baby girl named Bogumiła, when her younger son, Stefan, complained of being sick. He was tired and nauseated, so Melania took him from his bedroom to the kitchen and laid a blanket and pillow on top of a storage chest so that he could sleep by the warm stove. By the second day, the boy did not want to eat, so Melania took him to a local physician, who said that the problem was with his stomach and just prescribed him some children's crackers. By the third day, her son stopped talking completely, and when Melania asked him what hurt, he weakly opened his mouth to show her his throat.

Dmytro rushed to the physician's office on his bicycle and demanded the paperwork needed for an ambulance to come take Stefan to the hospital. He argued with the physician, who claimed that the boy was just acting sick to gain sympathy from his mother, before storming off to the post office to call for an ambulance himself. He then sped home and leaned the bicycle against the wall, jumping into the ambulance with his son as soon as it arrived. Melania, crying so hard that she could see nothing through her tears as they drove off, had no choice but to stay home to take care of the rest of her children. Only after Dmytro left did the mailman arrive at the house on Dmytro's bicycle, explaining how Dmytro had been so upset that he did not notice he was riding away on the mailman's bicycle, along with its basket for carrying letters, instead of his own.

Dmytro and Stefan arrived at the hospital in Kożuchów but were told that they had to go to another hospital in Nowa Sól, where they then were told that there was not enough room. They would need to go to yet a third hospital in Zielona Góra. They arrived in Zielona Góra by evening, only to be criticized by a female hospital worker for coming in so late. Fuming, Dmytro threatened to take the matter of his son's medical treatment to the local Communist Party officials if she did not help them. Dmytro did not belong to the Communist Party, but the hospital worker evidently did and suddenly began to speak to him more politely. She summoned a doctor to examine the boy, who arranged for him to be transferred to a hospital in Poznań that was better equipped. Dmytro did not return home to Jarogniewice until the following morning.

A few days later, Melania's older son, Petro, wanted nothing more than to climb into Dmytro's arms and to be near his father. Melania thought that Petro was just missing Stefan until he started to feel nauseated and developed a fever. Dmytro called an ambulance to take Petro to the hospital in Poznań right away. Melania, unable to banish the horrid thought from her mind that maybe their younger son had not survived, convinced Dmytro to borrow money from a friend in case they needed to pay to bury Stefan in Poznań. When the ambulance arrived, Petro kissed his mother good-bye, with naive excitement about going to join his brother. Melania was sure that Petro's legs were moving more stiffly than they had before as he walked with his father to the ambulance.

Petro and Stefan stayed in isolation, sometimes together, sometimes apart. Nobody, not even their parents, was allowed to visit them. Once when Hania came to the hospital, one of the nurses whom she knew from her treatment in Poznań let the boys, with white kerchiefs on their heads to keep them from getting cold, look at her standing outside through a window up above. The nurse seemed to regret it, however, when the boys started crying that they wanted to go home with their aunt. Dmytro and Melania called the hospital often to inquire about their sons' health but were always told that, although the boys were better, they were still not ready to go home. Melania made a promise to God that if her sons survived, she would give up meat every Friday.

Finally, after months passed, the hospital sent a telegram to Dmytro and Melania saying that they could come for their children. Dmytro traveled to Poznań with new clothing that Melania had sewn for the day when she hoped her sons would return. As soon as Petro and Stefan saw Dmytro, they jumped on him, wrapped their arms around his neck, and would not let go, Dmytro told Melania when he brought them home.

An unexpected but dear guest would visit, a Gypsy woman told Melania's brother Petro in Ukraine soon after his second daughter, Liliya, was born in September 1955. The Gypsy woman came begging to Petro's house in Stanisławów, so he gave her an old pair of shoes, and, in return, she read his palm. Petro scoffed at the prediction about the guest, but not long afterward, Seman sent word that he was coming from western Poland to Soviet Ukraine for a visit. Seman arrived in Stanisławów by train, missing a bag of goods that had been stolen on the way. Petro led him back to the cramped one-room apartment where he, Olya, and their daughters had been living and that Petro, working as a teacher, had finally purchased from the resettled Polish woman who never moved back to the Soviet Union. This was the first time in almost nine years that Seman and Petro were able to see one another.

With Nikita Khrushchev having taken over as the head of the Communist Party of the Soviet Union after Stalin's death, the political environment in the Soviet bloc was loosening up. Khrushchev began to speak about Stalin's past crimes within inner party circles, and the Stalinist faction in Poland fell out of favor with Moscow. Polish intellectuals called for reforms within the Soviet bloc, and Melania heard over the PGR loudspeakers how workers in cities like Poznań were being arrested at protests where they demanded better conditions from the Communist government. With the idea of a national form of Communism instead of the Soviet model dominating public discussions, Władysław Gomułka—a seemingly moderate leader willing to implement reforms but not sever relations with the Soviet Union—found support among the Polish Communists again, who chose him as first secretary of the Polish United Workers' Party in October 1956.

The Polish government also agreed to designate the Ukrainian population as an official minority and allow it to promote its culture under the auspices of the newly formed Ukrainian Social-Cultural Society, the UTSK. At conferences of the UTSK, Ukrainian representatives started to openly discuss their rights to return to their former residences, to establish Ukrainian schools, to study Ukrainian in Polish schools, to practice their religion, and to be involved in Polish political life. Ukrainian-language newspapers, like *Nasze Slowo*, began to be published. Moreover, in internal discussions, the Polish political elite began to voice criticism of the handling of Operation Vistula, such as the Ministry of Internal Affairs stating that not only was it wrong but that it had caused political harm and a deep resentment among those relocated.

Petro traveled back to Poland to visit his family in Troska for the first time at the end of the school year in 1957. He sent Olya and their two daughters ahead by train while he finished his work. Olya and the little girls had tickets as far as the city of Wrocław, Poland, where someone from Petro's family was supposed to meet them. Olya carried her baby, Liliya, and a suitcase filled with their clothes, while nine-year-old

Myroslava dragged another of their suitcases. They made sure to bring along some Soviet goods that could be traded for Polish items during their trip.

When they got off the train in Wrocław, however, nobody was there to meet them. Having traveled more than seven hundred kilometers, with no idea where to go next and no more than a few Polish coins, Olya sat down with her daughters on their suitcases to wait. Finally, she asked a station worker to make an announcement for her over the loudspeaker, and, moments later, she saw a young woman running toward her. It was Hania, who had been little Myroslava's age the last time Olya saw her. The women greeted each other excitedly, and Hania led Olya and the girls, hungry from the trip, to a restaurant in the train station. Sitting at a table in the restaurant, they laughed when they heard the announcement over the loudspeaker that a woman named Olya Pyrtej had traveled from the Soviet Union and was waiting for her party to meet her.

The females made their way by train and then by car to Troska, where Petro met them a few weeks later. As Petro embraced and kissed Maria and Hania at length, his daughters stood by waiting patiently, also wanting to say hello. Myroslava and Liliya had not seen their father for days, but as he greeted his mother and sister after twelve years, Petro's daughters would have to wait for his attention.

The Polish government was allowing Ukrainians to return to southeastern Poland, Melania and her family finally heard. In an attempt to regulate the number of people fleeing from the Recovered Territories, the Polish United Workers' Party had issued a resolution in April 1957 appointing a commission to develop "opportunities for individual and group returns of the Ukrainian population to the Lublin, Rzeszów, and Kraków Provinces." The resolution stipulated, however, that returns would only occur with the permission of the government and depended on whether the property of the interested person was available or had been given away but was not actually being used.

Seman, now an old man in his seventies, was beside himself, badly wanting to move back to his home in Smerekowiec. His family watched him hurry about, inquiring about the prospect of moving, trying to obtain a copy of his official *karta przesiedleńcza*—his relocation card, which listed all the information about his family's resettlement and what they left behind—and to pull together the paperwork necessary to request a return. Never mind that the Polish government had officially taken control of his property. Never mind that the Polish officials had given away his house to the *góralka*, who had burned the house down. Never mind that he might have to buy back all the property that he had owned.

A handful of Seman's old neighbors were returning to Smerekowiec, to houses in disrepair and to a destroyed community instead of to the tight-knit village of Lemkos they had left behind. Seman made a deal with one of his old neighbors who returned. He paid the man to plant potatoes on the Pyrtej family's former, now fallow, land, agreeing that they would be Seman's if he returned and the neighbor's if Seman did not. Seman kept telling his family that they would have their own potatoes when they all came back to Smerekowiec, but the family only humored him. As it turned out, Seman's old neighbor would keep all the potatoes that he planted for the Pyrtej family.

Seman paid a visit to Melania in Jarogniewice, trying to convince her to come with him and to move her family back to the Lemko region. Dmytro, no longer just a son-in-law in Seman's house, however, decided in conversations with Melania that he would not return to their homeland and the unknown that now existed there. Because of Operation Vistula he had no home or community to go back to. The Lemko region that they remembered and that Melania sometimes dreamed about—where they would meet with village friends in the evenings to entertain one another and sing while they did their work—no longer existed. By the late 1950s, only approximately three thousand Lemkos had returned. Dmytro, furthermore, did not want his children to have to leave school to help the family work in the fields, as Melania had to as a child, so that they could rebuild their farm. He resolved instead to move somewhere where they would no longer be punished for being the minority.

Dmytro had been making plans to move to the United States, where his older brother Stefan had immigrated as a young, single man, long before World War II ever started. Back then nobody else from their family had really considered leaving Smerekowiec for good; Dmytro and his other siblings had been too young. But now, with help from America,

Dmytro's younger brothers, Iwan and Roman, were departing Poland with their wives and children, and Dmytro figured that he and his family should try to leave as well.

In America—*v Hamerytsi*, as the Lemkos said—life would be better, Melania imagined. They would be able to find work and buy for themselves all the things, like nice clothes and bicycles, that Dmytro's brother had sent them over the years. They would be able to build a better life for themselves than on the collective farm, where Dmytro worked with men who were paid in liquor and where he had learned to drink with them in the barn, sometimes coming home so drunk that he immediately fell asleep on the bed. Melania knew that it would not be easy to start a life in a country where she and Dmytro, well past middle age, did not know the language; but she did not think that it would be harder for them than it had been in Poland.

Dmytro and Melania prepared for all the medical tests that they would need to immigrate to the United States. Dmytro stopped drinking and quit smoking to clear up the dark spot that had been found in his lungs. Melania fed him sweet cream and eggs every day to help him gain a healthy weight. With their five children they then traveled to Warsaw, where a doctor working for the American embassy examined the whole family. The doctor asked Melania whether any of her children had ever been seriously ill, but she knew better than to confess to anything, and they all passed their health exams.

Finally, on May 10, 1961, Dmytro, Melania, and their children said good-bye to their friends and relatives in Poland. The family stood outside their house in Jarogniewice with seven suitcases, one for each traveler. They were taking nothing with them except clothing, having sold or given away everything else. Wasyl had come by to see them the day before, making Melania promise that she would eat and not starve in America. Seman, Maria, and Hania came not long before the family had to leave for their train ride to Warsaw, from where they would fly to the United States. Dmytro's brother Stefan had already lent them the money to buy plane tickets. Melania hugged her mother and Hania, who shed tears over parting with the five young nieces and nephews she had helped raise. As they all said good-bye, Seman embraced Dmytro, telling him that he hoped they would remember only the good and not any of the bad.

Epilogue

The "Compensation"

More than fifty years after Operation Vistula, Hania began to hear talk about how Ukrainians in Poland could apply to the courts to reclaim ownership of the property from which their families had been evicted. Hania, already in her midsixties, was visiting a friend in Zielona Góra after church one Sunday when he told her about an article in the latest edition of the Ukrainian-language newspaper *Nasze Slowo*. The article described a man who in 1999 legally requested the repeal of the decision that had permitted the government to confiscate his grandmother's land in the Lemko region. Hania knew of the man, Stefan Hładyk, from community events like the Łemkowska Watra festival.

Mr. Hładyk's legal case pointed out that on July 27, 1949, the Communists governing Poland had passed a decree transferring all the property in southeastern Poland that was not in private use into the hands of the state, thereby depriving the relocated Ukrainian population of all rights to their former territory. Based on this decree, the Polish government confiscated eleven hectares of land that had belonged to Mr. Hładyk's grandmother Maria. Mr. Hładyk asked that the authorities repeal this postwar decision, meaning that he, as Maria's descendant, could rightfully recover his family's land. At first, Poland's Ministry of Agriculture accommodated his request. Then a Polish governmental agency known as the State Forests, which managed the country's wooded areas and officially owned the seven and a half hectares of Maria's land consisting of forest, appealed the ministerial decision. Poland's Supreme Administrative Court was reviewing the matter, but in the meantime Hładyk's case encouraged other victims of Operation Vistula to take action. Hania decided that she was going to try to recover her family's former land in Smerekowiec as well.

Hania felt she was the only person left from her immediate family who could demand compensation from the Polish government. Her father, Seman, despite his desire to return to the Lemko region, died in Troska in April 1964. Hania sent her siblings a telegram informing them of their father's death. Seman passed away almost three years after Hania's sister, Melania, and brother-in-law, Dmytro, immigrated with their children to the United States and a little more than a year after Hania got married to another Lemko living in Troska, Szymon Lozyniak, Dmytro's nephew, as fate would have it. Melania was the one who suggested Szymon as a possible match for Hania just before leaving Poland.

Hania's mother, Maria, remained in Troska for another decade or so along with the family's loyal farmhand, Wasyl, whom Hania always remembered entertaining her as a little girl by drawing pictures of goats on the endless pieces of paper that she brought him. After Hania and her husband built a new house in Kożuchów, though, Maria moved in with them, and Wasyl moved into an old age home until they both finally passed away. Hania sent a telegram to her siblings again in January 1979, this time about their mother's death. One by one, the inhabitants of Troska found better living conditions elsewhere until, eventually, the village became deserted. The local state-run collective farms removed all the bricks from the remaining houses in order to build homes for their workers in other towns, Hania heard. As the grass grew wild over the foundations of the former houses in Troska, hardly any sign remained that anyone, German, Ukrainian, or otherwise, ever lived there.

Hania's older brother, Petro, had also passed away just months earlier, in November 1999, in Ivano-Frankivsk, Ukraine. He and his wife, Olya, only returned to the Lemko region for the first time the year that Seman died, bringing along their two girls. Olya walked from Krynica to Tylicz with her daughters so that they could see the long path she had taken daily to the Ukrainian teachers' seminary. However, when they reached the edge of the garden that used to belong to her family, Olya's feet would not take her any farther, and she started to sob until a kind neighbor— a Lemko woman married to a Pole who had not had to relocate—took them all inside. Whereas Olya now found the Lemko region too

Epilogue

heartbreaking and never came back again, Petro would try to return and attend the annual Łemkowska Watra as often as possible, as if he wanted to breathe in as much of his homeland's air as he could to last him until the next visit. An academic to the end, he spent years compiling the material to create one of the few existing dictionaries of Lemko words but did not survive to witness its successful publication.

Melania was Hania's only living sibling, but she rarely had the opportunity to travel from the United States to Poland. Melania was unable to attend her father's funeral because she had not yet obtained American citizenship, allowing her to travel back and forth. Then she missed her mother's funeral because of bad weather that temporarily grounded her plane. As soon as Melania became an American in 1966— renouncing her Polish citizenship in the process, as did Dmytro and her children—she tried to bring Hania, Szymon, and their daughter, Lila, who was born the year before, to the United States. However, the Polish authorities informed Hania that there was a limitation on emigration, and they could not leave. The period of liberalization under Gomułka was ending as the Polish leader backtracked from his moderate stance, turning into an authoritarian leader who did not tolerate independent opinions and actions. By the time the Polish authorities would finally allow Hania to emigrate, her daughter and her second child, a boy named Roman, would already be settled in school, and Hania would not feel able to leave Kożuchów in order to start a new life across the ocean.

Even after decades of living in western Poland, Hania still vividly recalled when she was nine years old and Petro—who always loved to throw her up in the air, squealing with joy, when he came home—said good-bye to their tearful parents before resettling to Soviet Ukraine. She also recalled when she was eleven years old, evacuating with her parents during Operation Vistula, and caught sight of some unripened berries in their garden that she would never get to taste. The idea that she might now be able to get back her family's property consumed her.

Hania contacted a local government office for information in the Województwo Małopolskie, or Lesser Poland Province, where her family's former land in Smerekowiec was now located. The office told her that in order to file her legal request, she would need to provide a number of documents, including a copy of her family's relocation card from 1947, proof of their landownership in Smerekowiec, maps showing where their land had been located, proof that Hania was a descendant of the person in whose name the land had been registered, and a paper from court confirming the proof that she was a descendant. Despite the long list, Hania decided to compile the paperwork by herself instead of paying a lawyer to do it. She bought a green folder and carefully punched three holes into it so that it could hold all the papers without anything falling out.

When she told her family and friends about her plan, though, Hania could see that everyone thought it was ridiculous. She was *przemądrzała*, too smart for her own good, Hania's husband teased her in Polish—the language that had crept into their dialogue more and more ever since arriving in the Recovered Territories. How was she, an elderly woman with only a high school education and no legal knowledge, going to manage all the politics involved with reclaiming territory owned before World War II? Hania had always wanted to go on to university and had even traveled to Zielona Góra to take the entrance exams; but once there, she received a telegram saying that she should come home because her parents were sick. She went home, but it turned out that her parents just needed her to help gather the crops. For lack of money, she was never able to attend university after that, even though she was sure she could have graduated.

Others warned her that the Polish government would never let the victims of Operation Vistula take back their land, because that might lead other ethnic groups to do the same, like Germans who had been removed from the Recovered Territories or surviving Jews who had lost their property during the war. The upper house of Poland's parliament had stated on August 3, 1990, that "the Senate of the Polish Republic condemns Operation 'Vistula,' during which the principle of collective responsibility—a characteristic hallmark of totalitarian systems—was adopted," but the lower house, the Sejm, still had not officially condemned the 1947 relocation plan, the Ukrainian community complained.

The sitting presidents of Poland and Ukraine, Aleksander Kwaśniewski and Leonid Kuchma, had also signed a joint declaration on agreement and reconciliation on May 21, 1997, in which they listed Operation Vistula—as well as the spilled blood of Poles in Wołyń—among the tragic events in Polish-Ukrainian history. However, the question of compensation had not yet been resolved when, after signing the joint declaration, President Kuchma concluded: "Today, there are no unsolved problems in Ukrainian-Polish relations."

The two presidents, furthermore, had jointly placed flowers beside a monument to the Jaworzno concentration camp victims that was unveiled on May 23, 1998, in the area where the bodies of the dead had been dumped, no longer leaving their grave unmarked in the middle of the woods. Yet the monument left all the blame and responsibility with the postwar Communist regime through a dedication—in Polish, Ukrainian, and German—that said: "In memory of the Poles, Ukrainians, Germans, all the victims of Communist terror who suffered unjustly here, all those who were imprisoned, murdered, or died during the years 1945–1956 in the Central Work Camp of the Ministry of Public Security in Jaworzno. In eternal homage."

Hania made phone calls and wrote letters, sometimes pleading and sometimes pressuring, to track down and arrange the documents she needed. As the months passed and one summer turned into another, her green folder grew thicker and thicker.

She learned that the confiscation of her family's land in Smerekowiec after Operation Vistula contradicted a regulation that a Polish president had established back on March 22, 1928, which stated that the government was not allowed to take control of private citizens' land. Making the argument that the local government's administrative decision to acquire her father's property in Smerekowiec flagrantly violated this 1928 regulation, she typed out a legal appeal to the head of the Lesser Poland Province. She offered a list of reasons why the decision to acquire Seman's property could not be regarded as valid, including the fact that the government had never publicized or notified the affected residents of that decision, thereby denying her father the opportunity to appeal it. In view of such violations, she asked that her father's land be returned. Along with this typed appeal, Hania sent all the required documents to the local government office in the Lesser Poland Province in June 2001—with the exception of a copy of her family's relocation card from 1947, which she never found.

Hope grew when Hania learned that in October 2001 Stefan Hładyk won his court case, with Poland's Supreme Administrative Court turning down the State Forests' appeal and confirming Mr. Hładyk as the owner of his grandmother's former forested land. The international media hailed the decision as a precedent-setting verdict that admitted that the nationalization of properties in the Lemko region fifty years earlier was illegal.

For almost two years Hania received occasional letters from the Polish government, always asking for some sort of clarification about her paperwork. Had her family been given any land in western Poland in exchange for what they left in the Lemko region? If yes, had they paid for this land? Could she provide additional proof that she was a descendant of Seman Pyrtej, in whose name her family's property was registered? Hania responded patiently to each question.

Then, finally, on March 20, 2003—only weeks after Hania's husband, Szymon, had passed away—the local government office in the Lesser Poland Province mailed her a document marked "Decision RR.IV .HW.7716-1/54/02/03." Hania read the seven-page document written in heavy legal language but did not understand it at first. So she read it over and over again a few more times. The communication contained two different parts. The first part informed her that the Polish government was returning the approximately six hectares of forests that her family had owned in the Lemko region. The second part informed her that, although the rest of her family's property in Smerekowiec—including about twelve and a half hectares of fields—had been taken from them illegally, the Polish government could not return the remainder because of irreversible legal consequences relating to the fact that this property now belonged to a number of private individuals. Hania was victorious, but this victory was bittersweet.

At the same time as Poland negotiated to become a full-fledged member of the European Union, Hania continued her appeals to the Polish government to receive some sort of compensation for her family's farmland. For years, through the election of successive presidents and governments in both Poland and Ukraine, she filed additional legal requests. She turned to the district and then the provincial courts. She traveled across the country to attend court proceedings. But she would receive no further reparations, the Polish authorities told her. File a case in the international court of law in Strasbourg, lawyers advised, something that Hania did not think she had the money or the strength to do.

In the end, Hania reclaimed the six hectares of forested land and legally divided them into three parcels: two hectares for her own children; two hectares for her sister in the United States; and two hectares for the wife and children of her late brother, Petro, in Ukraine. The land belonged not just to her but to her siblings too, she believed—although Hania, Melania, and Petro would never return to live in Smerekowiec again, and the decision about how the idle forestland would be used would ultimately fall to their children and grandchildren. The postwar Soviet-Polish population exchange and Operation Vistula had forever destroyed the Lemko region that Hania had known as a child. Still, she had succeeded in saving at least a small piece of her homeland for the next generation of her family.

Acknowledgments

I am grateful, first of all, to the staff of the Polish-U.S. Fulbright Commission and specifically to its executive director, Andrzej Dakowski, who believed in my project to interview the survivors of Operation Vistula, setting me on the path to ultimately write this book. I also thank my professors at Johns Hopkins University's School of Advanced International Studies (SAIS), namely, Bruce Parrott, Ilya Prizel, and Zbigniew Brzezinski, and my supervisor at Jagiellonian University, Jarosław Moklak, for supporting my research as a Fulbright scholar.

Many others have helped me along the path to publication. I would not have completed this book without the guidance of Sam Freedman, whose Book Seminar I had the good fortune to take at Columbia University's Graduate School of Journalism. (Among Sam's numerous recommendations was that I read the novel *When the Emperor Was Divine* by Julie Otsuka about the internment of Japanese Americans during World War II, which gave me the inspiration to use short vignettes to tell this nonfiction narrative.)

I am also deeply indebted to Gwen Walker, my acquisitions editor at the University of Wisconsin Press, for seeing value in my book manuscript and offering me her invaluable wisdom throughout the publication process. I am equally indebted to other UW Press staff members, including Sheila McMahon (the editor whose attention to every detail got me to the finish line), Logan Middleton, Matthew Cosby, Adam Mehring, and Carla Marolt, for all of their hard work on my book, as well as to Mary Hill for the copyediting.

I would, furthermore, like to thank professors Leonid Heretz, Piotr Wróbel, and especially Frank Sysyn; friends Kim Jastremski and Brian

Ardan; and members of the Uptown Writers Group, including Lori Soderlind, Kathleen Crisci, and Sarah Durham, for taking the time to read and comment on early drafts of my manuscript. Likewise, I greatly appreciate the review of my manuscript by professors Andrzej Kamiński, Olga Linkiewicz, Jan Pisuliński, Marek Wierzbicki, and Andrzej A. Zięba during the tenth "Recovering Forgotten History: The Image of East-Central Europe in Anglo-Saxon Textbooks" conference in Poland in 2012.

My sincere thanks go as well to Peter Potichnyj for answering my many e-mail inquiries pertaining to the Ukrainian Insurgent Army (UPA); Myroslava Anna Diakun for her willingness to share with me copies of the diary and other documents compiled by her father, Mychajlo Fedak; Steve Kapitula for giving me copies of the documents kept by his father, Pawel Kapitula; Eugeniusz Misiło for helping me with information concerning the Jaworzno concentration camp; Danuta and Bohdan Skrypak, Vera and Maximilian Masley, and Antonina Mykhailovich Ivanova for hosting me in Poland, Canada, and Ukraine, respectively; David Lawrence and Peter Reilly for creating the maps and graphics in the book; and Blythe Woolston for helping to compile the index.

I am, additionally, appreciative of the financial assistance that the Shevchenko Scientific Society, Inc., provided to me, which permitted me to travel to Ukraine in 2010 to conduct oral interviews. Through the Volodymyr and Lydia Z. Bazarko Fellowship from Columbia University's Harriman Institute, I was also able to conduct archival research at the Instytut Pamięci Narodowej-Komisji Ścigania Zbrodni przeciwko Narodowi Polskiemu in Rzeszów, Poland, in 2006.

Finally, I will be forever thankful for the support and love that my family and friends gave me while I was developing this book. To Melania (Pyrtej) Lozyniak, Hania (Pyrtej) Lozyniak, Olya (Petryszak) Pyrtej, and all my other family members described in this book, I pray that I have done justice to the stories you shared with me. To my relatives from Ukraine and Poland, particularly Vira Velykoroda; Liliya, Bohdan, and Markiyan Tkhir; Lila Marciniuk; and Bartek Adamcio: thank you for answering my dozens of questions and requests. To Alastair Rabagliati, Andrew Stromberg, Myron Melnyk and Adrianna Melnyk Hankewycz, Rafal Rygula and Kamila Zoubkova, Mark Howansky and Mary Hrywna, Lena Howansky, and the rest of the extended Howansky,

Lozyniak, and Reilly clans, your words of encouragement and assistance along the way made all the difference. To Stella Langer, I am grateful for the time you spent babysitting Olivia while I worked.

Most of all, to my parents, Stefan (Steven)† and Mary Nadia Howansky, I hope that I can somehow repay all the help that you have given me and that I will be able to provide for my children even half as well as you have provided for me. And to my husband and best friend, Brian Reilly, without your eternal patience and kind heart (not to mention your computer skills!), this book would not have become a reality.

Notes

Introduction

ix banning the use of the Ukrainian language: Orest Subtelny, *Ukraine: A History* (Toronto: University of Toronto Press, 1988), 426–46.

x led to this becoming a common political tactic: Mark Kramer, introduction, 1–8, 18–21, and Philipp Ther, "A Century of Forced Migration: The Origins and Consequences of 'Ethnic Cleansing,'" 49–50, both in *Redrawing Nations: Ethnic Cleansing in East-Central Europe, 1944–1948*, ed. Philipp Ther and Ana Siljak (Lanham, MD: Rowman & Littlefield, 2001).

— wished to create a new order: Krystyna Kersten, "Forced Migration and the Transformation of Polish Society in the Postwar Period," in Ther and Siljak, *Redrawing Nations*, 76–77.

— expelled the German population: Stanisław Jankowiak, "'Cleansing' Poland of Germans: The Province of Pomerania, 1945–1949," 87–88, and Eagle Glassheim, "The Mechanics of Ethnic Cleansing: The Expulsion of Germans from Czechoslovakia, 1945–1947," 205, both in Ther and Siljak, *Redrawing Nations*.

— rounding up Americans of Japanese heritage: John Basarab, "Post-war Writings in Poland on Polish-Ukrainian Relations, 1945–1975," in *Poland and Ukraine, Past and Present*, ed. Peter J. Potichnyj (Edmonton: Canadian Institute of Ukrainian Studies, 1980), 252.

xi three different orientations: Jarosław Moklak, "The Political Situation of the Ruthenians of the Lemko Region before the Outbreak of WWII— Historical Conditions," in *The Lemko Region, 1939–1947: War, Occupation and Deportation*, ed. Paul Best and Jarosław Moklak (New Haven, CT: Carpatho-Slavic Studies Group, 2002), 19–23; Paul J. Best, "Moscophilism among the Lemko Population in the Twentieth Century," in *The Lemkos of Poland: Articles and Essays*, ed. Paul Best and Jarosław Moklak (New

Haven, CT: Carpatho-Slavic Studies Group, 2000), 55–59; and Paul J. Best, "The Lemkos as a Micro Ethnic Group," http://lemko.org/lih/intro.html.

xi ancestors of the Lemkos: Bohdan Horbal, *Lemko Studies: A Handbook* (New York: Columbia University Press, 2010), 1–2, 333–45; Roman Reinfuss, *Śladami Łemków* (Warsaw: Wydawnictwo PTTK "Kraj," 1990), 140–41; Zofia Szanter, "From Where Did the Lemkos Come?," in Best and Moklak, *The Lemkos of Poland*, 89–100.

— more influenced in the early twentieth century by the Ukrainian national movement: Paul Robert Magosci, "The Ukrainian Question between Poland and Czechoslovakia: The Lemko Rusyn Republic (1918–1920) and Political Thought in Western Rus'–Ukraine," *Nationalities Papers* 21, no. 2 (Fall 1993), http://www.carpatho-rusyn.org/lemkos/lemrepub.htm.

— Polish soldiers killing Lemko civilians: Jan Pisuliński, *Przesiedlenie ludności ukraińskiej z Polski do USRR w latach 1944–1947* (Rzeszów: Wydawnictwo Uniwersytetu Rzeszowskiego, 2009), 477.

xii the Lemkos should be evacuated: Eugeniusz Misiło, *Repatriacja czy deportacja: Przesiedlenie Ukraińców z Polski do USRR 1944–1946*, 2 vols. (Warsaw: Oficyna Wydawnicza "Archiwum Ukraińske," 1996), 2:45–49, 90–91, 102–3. Volumes 1 and 2 of *Repatriacja czy deportacja* contain copies of no fewer than 319 original archival documents in Polish and Ukrainian. In April 1946 the chief representative of the Polish government for the evacuation of the Ukrainian population, Józef Bednarz, sent the letter to the Polish Academy of Sciences requesting confirmation of the Lemkos' origins. He received a reply from a professor named Tadeusz Kowalski from Jagiellonian University. A few days later, the deputy minister of public administration, Władysław Wolski, wrote to Bednarz that the Lemkos should also be evacuated.

— to get rid of the entire Ukrainian minority: Eugeniusz Misiło, *Akcja "Wisła" 1947: Dokumenty i materialy* (Warsaw: Archiwum Ukraińskie & Management Academy Group, 2012), 5, 13 (this volume contains copies of 480 Polish archival documents); Grzegorz Motyka, *Od rzezi Wołyńskiej do Akcji "Wisła": Konflikt polsko-ukraiński 1943–1947* (Kraków: Wydawnictwo Literackie, 2011), 421–23; Timothy Snyder, *The Reconstruction of Nations: Poland, Ukraine, Lithuania, Belarus, 1956–1999* (New Haven, CT: Yale University Press, 2003), 195–98; Ther, "A Century of Forced Migration," 56–57, and Marek Jasiak, "Overcoming Ukrainian Resistance: The Deportation of Ukrainians within Poland in 1947," 183–86, in Ther and Siljak, *Redrawing Nations*. Much has been written about Operation Vistula; for analyses of historiographies of this literature, see Andrzej L. Sowa, "Akcja 'Wisła' w polskiej historiografii—Aktualne problemy badawcze," 12–25, and Ihor Iliuszyn, "Akcja 'Wisła' w historiografii ukraińskiej," 26–35, in *Akcja "Wisła,"* ed. Jan Pisuliński (Warsaw: Instytut Pamięci Narodowej, 2003).

xii This was ethnic cleansing: *Encyclopaedia Britannica Online*, s.v. "ethnic cleansing," http://www.britannica.com/EBchecked/topic/194242/ethnic-cleansing.

— Poland's cultural diversity deteriorated: Timothy Snyder, "Akcja 'Wisła' a homogeniczność społeczeństwa polskiego," in Pisuliński, *Akcja "Wisła,"* 49–54.

xiii "Any reconstructed narrative": Jack Hart, *Storycraft: The Complete Guide to Writing Narrative Nonfiction* (Chicago: University of Chicago Press, 2011), 221.

— "Millions of peasants": George Orwell, "Politics and the English Language," *Horizon* 13, no. 76 (April 1946): 252–65.

Prologue: The Realization

3 they always used the word *lem*: Horbal, *Lemko Studies*, 133; Roman Reinfuss, *Łemkowie jako grupa etnograficzna* (Sanok: Muzeum Budownictwa Ludowego w Sanoku, 1998), 17.

8 against archival materials: During the summer of 2006, I conducted research in the archives of the Instytut Pamięci Narodowej-Komisji Ścigania Zbrodni przeciwko Narodowi Polskiemu in Rzeszów, Poland. In September 2011 I reviewed materials about the Ukrainian Insurgent Army (UPA) that are housed in the Peter J. Potichnyj Collection on Insurgency and Counterinsurgency in Ukraine at the University of Toronto.

Chapter 1. Caught on the Battlefield of World War II

9 during the first days of September 1939: To establish all the events relating to World War II throughout this chapter, I relied on the Eastern Europe Timeline created by Worldwar-2.net at http://www.worldwar-2 .net/timelines/war-in-europe/eastern-europe/eastern-europe-index.htm.

10 instead demanded Zaolzie: Norman Davies, *God's Playground: A History of Poland*, 2 vols. (Oxford: Oxford University Press, 1981), 2:431.

— to invade the rest of Czechoslovakia: Magosci, *A History of Ukraine* (Seattle: University of Washington Press, 1996), 613–16. Subcarpathian Ruś, a region within Czechoslovakia that had gained autonomy after the implementation of the Munich Agreement and changed its name to Carpatho-Ukraine, declared independence but was quickly taken over by Hungary.

10 on the morning of September 1, 1939: Davies, *God's Playground*, 2:435–40.

11 Melania's father, Seman: The majority of the narrative relating to Seman Pyrtej and his wife, Maria, who passed away long before I was born, is based on my interviews with their oldest daughter, Melania Pyrtej Lozyniak, who had knowledge of his activities, confirmed where possible during interviews with their youngest daughter, Hania Pyrtej Lozyniak.

15 resettling minority groups: Joseph B. Schechtmann, "The Option Clause in the Reich's Treaties on the Transfer of Population," *American Journal of International Law* 38, no. 3 (1944): 356–74, http://www.jstor.org/stable/2192377.

21 formation of the Ukrainian Central Committee: Subtelny, *Ukraine*, 457–58, 470; Magosci, *A History of Ukraine*, 620; Ukrainian Canadian Research and Documentation Centre, http://www.ucrdc.org/HI-UKRAINIAN_CENTRAL_COMMITTEE.html.

— Ukrainian teachers' seminary would also be opening: Stepan Kishchak, *Ukraïns'ka uchytels'ka seminariia v Krynytsi* (Lviv, 2007), 3–17.

22 also followed the German troops into Soviet-occupied Ukraine: Subtelny, *Ukraine*, 463–65; Magosci, *A History of Ukraine*, 626.

24 leading hundreds of Jews into the Garbacz forest: International Association of Jewish Genealogical Societies International Jewish Cemetery Project, http://www.iajgsjewishcemeteryproject.org/poland/gorlice.html; JewishGen, http://www.shtetlinks.jewishgen.org/gorlice/gorlice_wartime_map.html. The extermination of Jews from the ghetto in Gorlice has been reported to have taken place on August 14, 1942.

— member of the anti-Nazi partisan unit: The fact that Petro Pyrtej was part of the anti-Nazi partisan unit led by Grzegorz Wodzik in the Gwardia Ludowa is confirmed by two testimonials, one by Michał Doński on November 16, 1996, and one by Stepan Olenycz on October 22, 1997. These testimonials were provided to the government of Ukraine so that Petro's wife, Olya, could receive government benefits provided to families who fought against Fascist Germany during World War II.

25 self-defense units to protect themselves from the Nazis: Jarosław Zwoliński, *Łemkowie w obronie własnej: Zdarzenia, fakty tragedie, wspomnienia z Podkarpacia* (Koszalin: Zakład Poligraficzny "Polimer," 1996), 15, 19, 24, 36–39, http://lemko.org/pdf/obrona.pdf; Horbal, *Lemko Studies*, 413–16. Horbal notes that non-Communist Polish underground organizations were also active in the Carpathians but that they did not seem to enjoy as much popularity among the Lemkos as the Communist movement.

26 Katyn Forest: Davies, *God's Playground*, 2:451–52, 487.

— named the National Homeland Council: Ibid., 2:467.

27 named the Polish Committee of National Liberation: Ibid., 2:556–57.

27   One of the first acts of the head of the Polish Committee of National Liberation: Misiło, *Repatriacja czy deportacja*, 1:17–19.

28   uprising would not only force the German army from Warsaw: Davies, *God's Playground*, 2:474–79.

30   a battle for the Dukla Pass: The Friends of Dukla Pass, http://www .dynamiclink.com/dukla/dukla_operation.htm; Club of Friends of the Military History of Slovakia (KPVHS), http://www.reenactment-sk.szm .com/Operations/Dukla.htm.

34   "The evacuation is voluntary": Misiło, *Repatriacja czy deportacja*, 1:31.

—   "will best solve the matter of nationality": Ibid., 1:40.

—   murderous interethnic conflict: Motyka, *Od rzezi Wołyńskiej*, 5–8, 447–48. The sensitivity of the Polish and Ukrainian nations to their past conflicts cannot be underestimated. As Motyka writes, the mass murder of Poles in Wołyń (Volhynia) and Eastern Galicia committed by individuals in the OUN and UPA between 1943 and 1945 is deeply rooted in the Polish historical consciousness, while the forced expulsion of Ukrainians from southeastern Poland in 1947 for the purpose of assimilating them remains a traumatic experience for the Ukrainian people. Motyka has stated that the goal of his publications is to convince the Ukrainians that the murder of Poles in Wołyń was a fact and to convince the Poles that Operation Vistula was not necessary. The massacres of Poles by Ukrainian nationalists in Wołyń (Volhynia) and Eastern Galicia, which Motyka details in his book *Od rzezi Wołyńskiej do Akcji "Wisła,"* are not described in *Scattered*'s narrative because they were outside the scope of the main characters' experiences and knowledge; but readers should understand that they greatly influenced the attitude of Poles toward Ukrainians in other regions such as western and northern Poland after World War II.

35   "The Bolsheviks always promise heaven" and "Stalin wants to evict us": Misiło, *Repatriacja czy deportacja*, 1:65.

—   first small battalion in eastern Lemko territory: M. Ripeckyj, ("*Horyslav*") Memoirs, box 82, folders 1–2, vol. 22, pp. 13–14, 19–22, Peter J. Potichnyj Collection on Insurgency and Counter-insurgency in Ukraine, Robarts Library, University of Toronto (hereafter cited as Potichnyj Collection); Peter Potichnyj, "The Lemkos in the Ukrainian National Movement," in Best and Moklak, *The Lemko Region*, 152–55, 163–66.

Chapter 2. The Reality of the Soviet-Polish Population Exchange

37   Provisional Government of the Republic of Poland: Davies, *God's Playground*, 2:479–80, 558.

38 conference in Yalta: Ibid., 2:487–88; S. M. Plokhy, *Yalta: The Price of Peace* (New York: Viking Penguin, 2010), chap. 30.

39 Marysia, the diminutive of Maria: Maria Nadia would later be known as Mary Nadia in the United States.

— tens of thousands of Ukrainians living in Polish counties closer to the border had already been resettled: Misiło, *Repatriacja czy deportacja*, 1:11.

— extended the terms of their population exchange agreement: Ibid., 1:10, 38, 78.

40 Ciechania, which had been completely destroyed: Natalia Klashtorna, "What Lemkos Say Is 'Their World': Its Image, Losses and Needs," in Best and Moklak, *The Lemko Region*, 225–26. In December 2010 I also traveled to the village of Michurine in the Donetsk Province in eastern Ukraine and interviewed individuals who had been resettled from the Lemko village of Ciechania at the end of World War II.

41 famous primitivist painter: *Nikifor* (Olszanica: BOSC s.c., 2000).

42 Lemkos converted to Orthodoxy: Jarosław Moklak, "The Phenomenon of the Expansion of Orthodoxy in the Greek Catholic Diocese of Przemysl: Missionary Activity of the Orthodox Church, 1918–1939," in Best and Moklak, *The Lemkos of Poland*, 116–17.

43 relief from paying taxes and opportunities to obtain credit: Misiło, *Repatriacja czy deportacja*, 1:31–32, 76.

— signed another agreement with Moscow on July 6: Ibid., 1:140–43.

— "To the inhabitants of the Lemko Region!": Ibid., 1:102.

— the true reason for resettlement: Ibid., 1:111.

44 was cultivating a new type of Lemko: Details concerning Mychajlo Fedak's activities in the Organization of Ukrainian Nationalists were taken from his personal diary, provided by his daughter Myroslava Anna Diakun (12–14).

— in the Lemko village of Mszana: Mychajlo Fedak completed his training at the Ukrainian teachers' seminary in the spring of 1943 (Peter J. Potichnyj, *Litopys UPA—Istoriia: Dokumenty i materiialy* [Toronto: Litopys UPA, 2005], 42:486). Mychajlo Fedak noted in his diary that he was arrested in April 1944 (14).

45 another man by the name of Mychajlo Fedak: Myroslava Anna Diakun, the daughter of Mychajlo Fedak (Smyrnyi), stated in an e-mail to me that Smyrnyi and Sokil were distantly related, going back four generations. She believes that the great-grandfathers of the two men were brothers. Ms. Diakun confirmed this information with Anna Mac, a sister of Smyrnyi. However, the authors Bohdan Halczak and Michal Šmigel have written that, based on information from Smyrnyj's other sister, Anastazja Cesarska, Smyrnyj and Sokil were not directly related despite bearing the same name and coming from the same village ("Działalność oddziału UPA Mychajło

Fedaka 'Smyrnego' na Łemkowszczyźnie, w latach 1945–48," Ukraińskie Towarzystwo Historyczne w Polsce, n. 17, http://uitp.net.pl/index.php/opra cowania/124-oddzial-upa-smyrnego-na-lemkowszczyznie).

45 became head of the seventh *raion*: Potichnyj, "Lemkos in the Ukrainian National Movement," 151. In November 1946 the seventh raion and eighth raion became the first raion and second raion of the OUN's newly created "Verkhovyna" nadraion. See Peter Potichnyj, "The Lemkos in the Ukrainian National Movement during and after WWII," a paper presented at the Twentieth National Convention of AAASS, November 18–21, Honolulu, Hawaii, box 151, folder 75, Potichnyj Collection; Misiło, *Akcja "Wisła" 1947*, 1156–57.

46 Ukrainian police officers abusing the locals: Mychajlo Fedak's diary, 2–7.

48 "Be well, my homeland": Lyrics confirmed in the CD *Immigrant* by Julia Doszna, produced by Brian Ardan and American Historical Recordings in 2005, http://www.folk.pl/folk/Zespoly/Szczegoly.php?Doszna4.

49 delays because of a lack of trains: Misiło, *Repatriacja czy deportacja*, 1:168.

— hosted a delegation of representatives of the Ukrainian population in Poland at a conference: Ibid., 1:143–44, 147–55.

50 Doński and the delegation members told the ministry: Ibid., 1:156–57.

— All that they asked: Ibid., 1:157–58.

53 proposal to use the military: Grzegorz Mazur, "Soviet Policy Concerning Resettlement of the Ukrainian Inhabitants of Polish Lands during and after WWII (1939–1936)," in Best and Moklak, *The Lemko Region*, 61–65; Pisuliński, *Przesiedlenie ludności ukraińskiej*, 298–302; Misiło, *Akcja "Wisła" 1947*, 41–42, 44. The representative of the Soviet government who was responsible for the relocation of the Ukrainian population from Poland was named Mykola Pidhornyj.

54 extending the population exchange further: Misiło, *Repatriacja czy deportacja*, 1:182.

— prolonged registration for the population exchange until the end of the year: Ibid., 1:10, 224–27.

— decreed that adopting a new faith did not in any way change one's nationality: Ibid., 1:131, 230–31; and Mazur, "Soviet Policy," 60–61.

— citing security as the reason: Misiło, *Repatriacja czy deportacja*, 1:255.

56 Lemko families relocated to the Soviet Union were starting to return: Ibid., 1:279–81.

57 began to include the word "Łemkowie": Misiło, *Repatriacja czy deportacja*, 2:50–51, 57–59; Roman Drozd, "Lemkos and the Resettlement Action to Soviet Ukraine (1944–1946)," in Best and Moklak, *The Lemko Region*, 86.

— aggravating the resistance of the Lemkos: Misiło, *Repatriacja czy deportacja*, 1:290–91.

— as a traitor: Ibid., 1:192.

57 "let the enemy know": Ibid., 1:200–201; Jan Pisuliński, "The Resettlement of Lemkos to the USSR and the Activities of the UPA in the Lemko Region in the Light of Documents Found in the [Polish] State Archives in Rzeszow," in Best and Moklak, *The Lemko Region*, 139–41. Grzegorz Motyka notes, however, that in the course of their actions in Poland in 1946, the Ukrainian partisans were forbidden from killing Polish civilians, although some often fell victim. On the other hand, the Polish military also killed innocent citizens while trying to pacify the UPA, such as in January 1946 in the village of Zawadka Morochowska, where dozens of men, women, and children were murdered. See Grzegorz Motyka, "Ukraińska Powstańcza Armia a akcja 'Wisła,'" in Pisuliński, *Akcja "Wisła,"* 111, 113.

—   prolonging the end of the relocation campaign until June 15: Misiło, *Repatriacja czy deportacja*, 1:296–98.

—   the Polish army beat and killed people: Pisuliński, *Przesiedlenie ludności ukraińskiej*, 391.

59 orders to increase the speed of evacuation: Misiło, *Repatriacja czy deportacja*, 2:106.

—   GO Rzeszów: "GO" stands for Grupa Operacyjna, or Operational Group.

—   in a bakery then run by the Lemko activist Michał Doński: Misiło, *Repatriacja czy deportacja*, 1:100.

—   asked him to help put an end: Ibid., 2:75–78.

60 Gomułka then wrote a letter on April 19: Ibid., 2:103–4. The representative to whom Gomułka wrote was Deputy Minister of Public Administration Władysław Wolski.

—   the Polish army was hauling off people: Ibid., 2:154–55.

—   482,107 individuals had been resettled from Poland: In his book, Prof. Jan Pisuliński clarifies that, although both the Polish and Soviet sides stated that 482,107 people had been resettled to the Soviet Union, this number does not include those Ukrainians and other ethnicities who were resettled from Poland first to Belarus and then to Ukraine, making the number closer to 494,805. He also notes that the actual percentage of Ukrainians who remained in Poland is impossible to determine for sure, but that it was much larger than the Polish authorities estimated. Pisuliński, additionally notes that, in comparison to those resettled to the Soviet Union, the official number of people resettled from Soviet Ukraine to Poland was about 792,700 individuals (Pisuliński, *Przesiedlenie ludności ukraińskiej*, 505, 507–8). Although *Scattered* focuses on the consequences of the Polish government's policies toward the Ukrainian minority, the bilateral character of the Soviet-Polish population exchange must be emphasized, as Poles were forced to evacuate from the Soviet Union as well, leaving the lands they had inhabited for centuries and moving to regions in Poland that were completely foreign to them.

61 push them to join the bands of Ukrainian nationalists: Misiło, *Repatriacja czy deportacja*, 2:162.

— "The Ukrainian (Lemko) population about whom there exists any reservations": Ibid., 2:270.

Chapter 3. Operation Vistula: The Solution to the "Ukrainian Problem"

81 never really understood how its members expected to create an independent Ukraine: In his memoirs from 1947 and 1948, the UPA leader Stepan Stebel's'kyi (code name Khrin) noted the difficulty in convincing Lemkos to support the UPA's struggle for Ukrainian independence, writing: "It was very difficult to recruit Lemkos. The Lemko was tied to his village, and was distrustful. But once he knows somebody, begins to love him, he will follow him even into fire. At first I went to Lemko villages, called meetings, made them nationally conscious by telling them that they were a famous princely tribe, that the enemy wanted to throw them out from their native land, and that they should defend themselves with weapons. I attended Lemko festivities, funerals, weddings. I listened to their griefs, complaints, desires, and requests. Then I brought it all to one point, the need to take up arms and use them in self-defense. . . . I began recruiting only when I felt that the population was on my side. . . . In order to bring Lemkos to my side, my slogan was 'we will defend our villages!' . . . Only after several months did I begin to talk about defending the entire territory of Lemkivshchyna. Afterward, I broadened their political horizon to Ukraine as a whole, stating as the main goal of our struggle the statehood and unity of our lands" (Stepan Stebel's'kyi, *Zymoiu v bunkri: Spohady—khronika 1947/1948* [Munich, 1950], 129; see also Litopys UPA online, http://www.litopysupa.com/main.php?pg=2&bookid=30).

— the UPA soldiers' strategy: Misiło, *Repatriacja czy deportacja*, 2:299.

82 in the nearby village of Klimkówka: Pisuliński, "The Resettlement of Lemkos," 142, 145; "Urząd Bezpieczeństwa Publicznego w Gorlicach, Nr. 581/46, 8.8.1946 do Szefa Wojewódzkiego Urzędu Bezpieczeństwa Publicznego w Rzeszowie: Raport sytuacyjny za okres od dnia 28.7.46 r. do dnia 7.8.1946 r.," Instytut Pamięci Narodowej-Komisji Ścigania Zbrodni przeciwko Narodowi Polskiemu, Rzeszów, Poland.

— Smyrnyi had also recently torched houses: Details concerning Mychajlo Fedak's activities are taken from his "Dennyk z dij UPA na Zachidnij

Lemkiwszczyni" (Daily record of the activities of UPA in Western Lemkiv-shchyna), provided by his daughter Myroslava Anna Diakun.

82 numbering over one hundred people: Potichnyj, *Litopys UPA—Istoriia*, 42:486; Grzegorz Motyka, "Ukraińska Powstańcza Armia a akcja 'Wisła,'" in Pisuliński, *Akcja "Wisła,"* 115.

84 tried to renew the population exchange: Misiło, *Repatriacja czy deportacja*, 2:8; Pisuliński, *Przesiedlenie ludności ukraińskiej*, 502–3.

85 reports of the Polish army beating people: Misiło, *Repatriacja czy deportacja*, 2:334, 338, 340.

— as the Polish Communists now referred to the western and northern terri-tories: Davies, *God's Playground*, 2:489, 518. The term "Recovered Territories" was official jargon used following World War II, as Poles were encouraged to believe that the eastern German land given to Poland was a return of their Motherland's territory from the medieval Piast period and that Poland had always had the right to inhabit these recovered lands.

— "The security of the border territory": Misiło, *Repatriacja czy deportacja*, 2:344–48; Misiło, *Akcja "Wisła" 1947*, 30, 106–12. There is debate over the role of the Soviet Union in the Polish Communist government's decision to carry out Operation Vistula and whether or not orders came from Mos-cow. While scholars such as Misiło have stated that no archival documents have yet been found to prove that Moscow pressured the Polish govern-ment to carry out Operation Vistula, other scholars like Ryszard Torzecki have maintained that Poland's Communist leadership after World War II remained subservient to the Soviet Union. Ryszard Torzecki stated that Stalin, wishing to destroy the Ukrainian independence movement, summoned Boleslaw Bierut to Moscow as early as October 1944 to discuss the battle against all forms of "counterrevolution" in Poland and that the Polish Communists simply acted as the implementers of Stalin's nationalities policy ("Wisła Zaczeła Się w Moskwie," *Gazeta Wyborcza*, May 20, 1997). It can also be debated whether Ostap Steca, the coauthor of many of the documents of the General Staff of the Polish army relating to Operation Vistula, was a Soviet plant in the Polish army who followed orders from Moscow and made sure they were carried out in Poland.

— from fighting the UPA to eliminating opposition candidates: Grzegorz Motyka has stated that during the winter of 1946–47 there was a chance for the Polish government to conduct military action against the UPA without resorting to ethnic cleansing in southeastern Poland. This would have been more difficult without resettlement but possible given the small amount of territory the UPA covered. However, the Polish government did not carry out such a military action because it did not consider the UPA a nationwide threat. Instead, it sent three-quarters of its military forces deployed in the areas covered by the UPA to falsify the parliamentary election results. The Polish government decided to resolve its problem with the Ukrainian partisans through resettlement not merely to liquidate the UPA but to dispense with the problem of the Ukrainian minority. See Grzegorz Motyka, "Ukraińska Powstańcza Armia a akcja 'Wisła,'" in Pisuliński, *Akcja "Wisła,"* 113–14.

85 the Provisional Government of National Unity was dissolved: Davies, *God's Playground*, 2:570–72. That February, Józef Cyrankiewicz was sworn in as the new prime minister, replacing Edward Osóbka-Morawski.

86 compile information about the number of Ukrainians who remained: Misiło, *Akcja "Wisła" 1947*, 213.

— "Since the Soviet Union will no longer accept these people": Ibid., 231–33.

— both Mossor and Steca attended a meeting: Ibid., 75, 251, 254–56. Misiło believes that also discussed at this meeting was a plan, named Operacja R or Operacja Rzeszowska, to liquidate the UPA and resettle the Ukrainian population that was supporting it, which was developed separately by Poland's Korpus Bezpieczeństwa Wewnętrznego, or Internal Security Corps, also in the period before March 21, 1947.

87 Gen. Karol Świerczewski, the Polish vice minister of national defense: Ibid., 295–98, 335–45. Except where noted, the description of General Świerczewski's assassination was re-created from government investigative reports dated April 11 and 17, 1947. Some of these details are also noted in Grzegorz Motyka's book *Tak było w Bieszczadach: Walki polsko-ukraińskie 1943–1948* (Warsaw: Oficyna Wydawnicza Volumen, 1999), 382–84.

— underground hospitals: Underground report, "1947 rik v Skhidnii Lemkivshchyni," box 51, folder 29, p. 13, Potichnyj Collection.

88 The shots were fatal: Zbigniew Kresek, *Szlak im. Gen. Karola Świerczewskiego w Bieszczadach: Przewodnik turystyczny* (Warsaw: Wydawnictwo PTTK "Kraj," 1985), 25. The sketch provided that relates to Świerczewski's assassination is based on a drawing done by Col. Jan Gerhard, one of the eyewitnesses who experienced the attack.

90 another diversionist group had made it look: The death of Świerczewski has been surrounded by controversy, including whether UPA soldiers were responsible for killing the general. A special committee made up of officers from Poland's Department of Security, or Urząd Bezpieczeństwa (UB), was created to look into the murder of Świerczewski and on April 17, 1947, provided a statement asserting that, while the committee was unable to apprehend the assassins, it accepted that the UPA had organized the attack. The committee based this assumption on evidence that during the attack

Polish soldiers heard commands being given in the Ukrainian language as well as the "battle cries 'urraa,' which are characteristic of UPA bands" (Misiło, *Akcja "Wisła" 1947*, 77–84, 213–16, 341). However, other authors such as Grzegorz Motyka have offered the possibility that Świerczewski was actually eliminated by either the Department of Security or the Soviet NKVD (predecessor of the KGB). Although Motyka has written that it is not clear whether the Polish or Soviet secret services would have killed Świerczewski because of his ties to Spain, because of the Soviet purges that were taking place at the time, or because a pretext was needed for Operation Vistula, Motyka has suggested intraparty intrigue (*Tak było w Bieszczadach*, 387–88).

90 "On March 28th of this year": Misiło, *Akcja "Wisła" 1947*, 258.

— decided to take repressive actions against the entire Ukrainian population: Ibid., 260–61.

91 the Polish minister requested that their mutual borders be closed: Ibid., 304–5.

— commanded by General Mossor: Ibid., 292.

— "Once and for all to solve the Ukrainian problem in Poland": Ibid., 312–15. See also *Aktsiia "Visla" 1947* (Warsaw-Kyiv: Instytut Pamięci Narodowej, 2006), 66–70, which is volume 5 of *Polska i Ukraina w latach trzydziestych—czterdziestych XX wieku*.

— the code name of the relocation plan changed to Akcja Wisła: Misiło, *Akcja "Wisła" 1947*, 311.

— to be kept in the strictest confidence within the military: Ibid., 331.

92 "the relocation operation of the Ukrainian population began": Ibid., 474–75.

— The first transport, number R-10: Ibid., 503–4, 1065.

93 completed their population exchange: Ibid., 550–52. This final protocol regarding the completion of the Soviet-Polish population exchange was signed on May 6, 1947.

— Returning from a visit to Gorlice: Ibid., 124, 653–54. The relocation via Operation Vistula of people of the Lemko region began on May 26, 1947. Reports show that the Sixth infantry division of the Polish Army was responsible for the relocation of the Lemko region.

95 to avoid negative treatment of the population: Ibid., 332–33.

97 hundreds of residents evacuated from Smerekowiec: Ibid., 1031.

101 their train, marked R-253, pulled out of Zagórzany: Ibid., 1070; Jerzy Żurko, *Rozsiedlenie ludności w ramach akcji "Wisła" w dawnym województwie wrocławskim* (Wrocław: Wydawnictwo Uniwersytetu Wrocławskiego, 2000), 43–44, 220–21.

102 arresting them for working with the Ukrainian nationalists: Misiło, *Akcja "Wisła" 1947*, 121–22, 353, 356.

Chapter 4. Prisoners in the Central Labor Camp in Jaworzno

106 "hostile and uncertain elements": Misiło, *Akcja "Wisła" 1947*, 403–6.

— from their homes and local churches: During my time as a Fulbright grantee in Poland, I interviewed a woman by the name of Zofia Smereczniak who was arrested by the Polish authorities as she went to place flowers in Saint Norbert's, the Ukrainian Catholic Church in Krakow, and was then taken to the Central Labor Camp in Jaworzno. Saint Norbert's was apparently suspected to be a contact point for the OUN/UPA, and Communist secret police set a trap for couriers there.

— his sister-in-law's uncle, Pawel Kapitula: Pawel Kapitula, interview by the author, April 10, 1998, Yonkers, NY. I wrote the chapter on the Central Work Camp in Jaworzno based on my interview with him, with the exception of the additional details cited in these notes. Mr. Kapitula emigrated from Poland to the United States in 1966 and passed away in Yonkers on May 16, 2001, at the age of eighty-nine (TheJournalNews.com, http://www.nyj news.com/obituary/obit.php3?id=516707).

107 arresting other suspected villagers: During my 1995 interview with Pawel Kapitula, he named several individuals from Żdynia who were arrested at the same time as he was. I cross-referenced this interview with the archive-based information about Jaworzno that I received from Eugeniusz Misiło, and I believe these individuals included Teodor Dziamba, Teodor Jedynak, and Szymon (Seman in the Lemko vernacular) Padła.

108 military courts for trial: Misiło, *Akcja "Wisła" 1947*, 617–18.

109 approximately eight kilometers: Ibid., 608.

— a sign read Centralny Obóz Pracy w Jaworznie: Stefan Dziubyna, *I stverdy dilo ruk nashykh: Spohady* (Warsaw: Oficyna Wydawnicza Archiwum Ukraińskie, 1995), 89.

— satellite of the Auschwitz camp: The history of the concentration camp in Jaworzno was found in sources such as Misiło, *Akcja "Wisła" 1947*, 151–57; "Historia obozu w Jaworznie," in *Między sąsiadami: Almanach Fundacji Świętego Włodzimie rza Chrzciciela Rusi Kijowskiej* (Kraków: Szwajpolt Fiol, 1998), 8:222–23; Jarosław Czuchta, "Religious Life and Interfaith Relations in the Lemko Region in the First Half of the 20th Century (to 1947)," in Best and Moklak, *The Lemko Region*, 215; Łukasz Kamiński, "Obóz Jaworzno: Ukraiński etap," in Pisuliński, *Akcja "Wisła,"* 174–76.

109 concentration camps for those Ukrainians considered a threat: Misiło, *Akcja "Wisła" 1947*, 267.

— begin mass arrests of suspected Ukrainian civilians: Ibid., 427–28.

110 June 13, 1947: Misiło, archive-based information about Jaworzno. This was less than three weeks before the Polish parliament passed an act creating the Auschwitz-Birkenau State Museum on July 2, 1947 (Misiło, *Akcja "Wisła" 1947*, 153).

— inmate number 1712: I received information from the scholar Eugeniusz Misiło that he compiled on the basis of various archival documents and is preparing for publication in a book about Jaworzno in which Pawel Kapitula's and Damian Howansky's camp numbers are listed.

— inhabited five barracks: Dziubyna, *I stverdy dilo ruk nashykh*, 90.

— small children: Iryna Bida, an inmate at the Central Labor Camp in Jaworzno who gave birth to her son while imprisoned, interview by Mychajlo Kozak, June 2, 1990, Toronto.

— gray camp uniform: As a Fulbright grantee in Poland in the spring of 1999, I interviewed a couple in the city of Legnica by the name of Petro and Maria Tkaczyk who met while imprisoned in the Central Labor Camp in Jaworzno. Mr. and Mrs. Tkaczyk corroborated many of the details of the camp noted throughout this chapter that Pawel Kapitula and other inmates described. In September 2011 I also met in Toronto with Maria Fedak (née Bajus), who was imprisoned in Jaworzno and confirmed the color of the camp uniforms worn by the prisoners.

111 who admitted to being in the Ukrainian insurgency: Dziubyna, *I stverdy dilo ruk nashykh*, 91.

— liquidate these groups quickly and completely: Misiło, *Akcja "Wisła" 1947*, 783–84.

— illegally returned to their former places: Ibid., 821–22.

— executed on the same day: Ibid., 654.

112 beat older inmates who lagged behind: Ivan Lyko, "Tiurma Montelupich and KZ. Jaworzno," box 90, folder 25, p. 30, Potichnyj Collection.

— throw the shoes outside: Petro and Maria Tkaczyk, interview.

— metal bowl: Dziubyna, *I stverdy dilo ruk nashykh*, 92; Petro and Maria Tkaczyk, interview.

— Scabies and typhus spread: Dziubyna, *I stverdy dilo ruk nashykh*, 95.

— solitary confinement: Ibid., 96.

— mental torment: Petro and Maria Tkaczyk, interview.

113 a man by the name of Węgrzyn: Misiło, *Akcja "Wisła" 1947*, 485. In the archival material that Misiło has gathered about Jaworzno, it is noted that a man by the name of Stefan Węgrzyn, the son of Aleksander and Maria,

born on January 9, 1909, in Wola Piotrowa, was arrested on May 7, 1947, arrived from Sanok to the Central Labor Camp in Jaworzno on May 22, 1947, and, according to the testimonies of other inmates, was known to serve the function of a *kapo* or *gońcem*, a prisoner functionary who carried out tasks for the Polish guards.

114 More than two dozen priests: Dziubyna, *I stverdy dilo ruk nashykh*, 94; Włodzimierz Mokry, "Ukraińcy w Jaworznie," in *Problemy Ukraińców w Polsce po wysiedleńczej akcji "Wisła" 1947 roku* (Kraków: Wydawnictwo "Szwajpolt Fiol," 1997), 83.

— accusations that he was distributing Ukrainian propaganda: Dziubyna, *I stverdy dilo ruk nashykh*, 55–56, 250.

— the Department of Security detained him: Ibid., 87–89.

115 numbered 1 through 7: Misiło, archive-based information about Jaworzno.

— Ukrainian inmates felt that the Germans: Dziubyna, *I stverdy dilo ruk nashykh*, 94. The perception that German prisoners in the Central Work Camp in Jaworzno were treated better than Ukrainian prisoners was expressed not only by Father Dziubyna in his book but also during interviews with Pawel Kapitula and Petro and Maria Tkaczyk.

116 assist the German doctors: Dziubyna, *I stverdy dilo ruk nashykh*, 95, 98. During my interview with Petro Tkaczyk, he discussed receiving better food while working in the German hospital.

— exhausted body gave birth: Bida, interview.

— also began to receive packages: The issue of Ukrainian prisoners receiving packages was mentioned in my interviews with both Pawel Kapitula and Petro and Maria Tkaczyk. See also Łukasz Kamiński, "Obóz Jaworzno: Ukraiński etap," in Pisuliński, *Akcja "Wisła,"* 176, where the author cites a quotation from Lt. Col. Oskar Karliner—who notoriously oversaw the cases of the Ukrainian prisoners in Jaworzno—saying that approval to give packages to the prisoners of the Central Labor Camp in Jaworzno was not always honored.

117 made identification cards: Dziubyna, *I stverdy dilo ruk nashykh*, 99.

— he died within a few days: Misiło, *Akcja "Wisła" 1947*, 1104. Misiło's book notes that Stefan Chrystyna, inmate number 1937, died on December 3, 1947.

— On January 5, 1948: Misiło, archive-based information about Jaworzno.

— to sign a document agreeing to keep secret: Dziubyna, *I stverdy dilo ruk nashykh*, 102. The issue of signing documents promising not to speak of their experiences in Jaworzno was mentioned not only by Petro and Maria Tkaczyk but also by Pawel Kapitula and Father Dziubyna.

118 3,873 Ukrainians imprisoned: Misiło, *Akcja "Wisła" 1947*, 155.

Chapter 5. A New Home
in the Recovered Territories?

120 other former inhabitants of Smerekowiec: The names of and stories about the people who traveled to Troska by truck, such as Marko Astrab and Pawlo Pupczyk, were provided by Melania Pyrtej Lozyniak.

122 could not exceed 10 percent: Misiło, *Akcja "Wisła" 1947*, 766.

125 jailed for returning illegally: Ibid., 224–25. Writing that it is difficult to gauge how many people tried to return to their former place of residence but that some people were determined to, Igor Hałagida noted that the primitivist painter Nikifor returned to his home of Krynica three times before the authorities finally allowed him to remain there. See Igor Hałagida, "Pierwsze lata Ukraińców na zachodnich i północnych ziemiach Polski po przedsiedleniu w ramach akcji 'Wisła' (1947–1952)," in Pisuliński, *Akcja "Wisła,"* 133.

126 remove all Poles from Ukrainian lands: Snyder, *Reconstruction of Nations*, 166–72. The Ukrainian archivist Volodymyr Viatrovych has argued that although individual members of Ukrainian nationalist groups were involved in killing Polish citizens in the Wołyń region for reasons including self-defense against German and Polish attacks, organizations such as the OUN and UPA did not officially promote a wider anti-Polish campaign or the policy of liquidating the Polish population. Volodymyr Viatrovych, *Druha pol's'ko-ukrains'ka viina, 1942–1947* (Kyiv: Vydavnychyi dim "Kyievo-Mohylians'ka akademiia," 2011), 113–19, 123, 125–26).

— had reported massacres: Motyka, *Od rzezi Wołyńskiej*, 109–50.

128 local Polish authorities monitored the Ukrainian population: Hałagida, "Pierwsze lata Ukraińców," 134, 139; and Hałagida, *Ukraińcy na zachodnich i północnych ziemiach Polski 1947–1957* (Warsaw: Instytut Pamięci Narodowej, 2003), 69. Hałagida writes about the monitoring of Ukrainian deportees at all times by organizations such as the Urząd Bezpieczeństwa (Department of Security), Milicja Obywatelska (Citizens' Militia), and Ochotnicza Rezerwa Milicji Obywatelskiej (Voluntary Militia Reserve). These works provide a great deal of detail about the life of Ukrainian deportees in the Recovered Territories.

— By the time the last transport of Ukrainians arrived: Misiło, *Akcja "Wisła" 1947*, 119, 1076.

— between 140,000 and 150,000 Ukrainians: Ibid., 25, 130–31, 1051, 1073, 1083–84. Misiło notes that, according to the State Repatriation Office, 140,660 Ukrainians were relocated during Operation Vistula; however, other information lists the number alternatively at 140,627 and 147,175, and the true number is likely not more than 150,000 Ukrainians.

129 became property of the state: Ibid., 932–34.

— release of prisoners from the Jaworzno concentration camp: Horbal, *Lemko Studies*, 432.

130 were sentenced to death: Misiło, *Akcja "Wisła" 1947*, 344.

— ordering most of its squadrons there to demobilize: Magosci, *A History of Ukraine*, 648-49; Subtelny, *Ukraine*, 490-91.

— make his way to the American zone: Chernyk-Smyrnyi (Mykhailo Fedak) Zvit nr. 25.10.1948. 2pp., box 184, folder 16, Potichnyj Collection. Iryna Tymochko-Kaminska, who became a leader of OUN's "Verkhovyna" nadraion under the codename "Khrystia," notes in her memoirs that she was responsible for informing members of the "Verkhovyna" nadraion about its liquidation, and that she and Smyrnyi had a heated exchange because he felt the order to leave was unfair to the members of the Ukrainian underground, who had fought to protect their homes day after day. Iryna Tymochko-Kaminska, *Moya Odyseya* (Warsaw: Oficyna Wydawnicza UKAR, 2005), 180-81.

131 Maria Bajus: "Baius, Maria, Biography," box 184, folder 16j, 5 pp., Potichnyj Collection; Misiło, *Akcja "Wisła" 1947*, 684.

— growing struggle among the Communists in Poland: Davies, *God's Playground*, 2:573-77.

— government could also now take possession: Ibid., 2:494-97.

— others tried the legal route: Tomasz Kalbarczyk, "Powrót Łemków," *Biuletyn Instytutu Pamięci Narodowej*, nos. 1-2 (2005): 66.

132 turn against and issue long-term sentences to military leaders: Misiło, *Akcja "Wisła" 1947*, 96, 219.

133 Immediate changes needed to be made: Roman Drozd and Igor Hała-gida, *Ukraińcy w Polsce, 1944–1989* (Warsaw: Burchard Edition, 1999), 65–66.

135 girl named Bogumiła: Years later, Bogumiła changed her first name to Stella.

137 Władysław Gomułka—a seemingly moderate leader: Davies, *God's Playground*, 2:582-84.

— newly formed Ukrainian Social-Cultural Society: Drozd and Hałagida, *Ukraińcy w Polsce*, 13, 79-81.

— Polish political elite began to voice criticism: Kalbarczyk, "Powrót Łemków," 71.

138 opportunities for individual and group returns: Drozd and Hałagida, *Ukraińcy w Polsce*, 106-7.

139 three thousand Lemkos had returned: Paul Robert Magosci, "The Lemko Rusyns: Their Past and Present," *Carpatho-Rusyn American* 10, no. 1 (1987), http://www.carpatho-rusyn.org/lemkos/lemkos2.htm.

Epilogue: The "Compensation"

141 Supreme Administrative Court was reviewing the matter: "Dostaną lasy albo pieniądze," *Rzeczpospolita*, no. 230, October 2, 2001, http://www.lemko .org/rzeczpospolita/hladyk.html.

144 "Senate of the Polish Republic condemns Operation 'Vistula'": "Polish Senate Resolution Condemns 1947 Resettlement of Ukrainians," *Ukrainian Weekly*, no. 33, Sunday, August 19, 1990, 1, 6.

— joint declaration on agreement and reconciliation: Michael Melnik, "Ukraine: Kuchma, Kwasniewski Sign Reconciliation Deal," translated from Moscow ITAR-TASS, FBIS Transcribed Text Daily Report, May 21, 1997.

146 precedent-setting verdict: Radio Free Europe/Radio Liberty, "Ethnic Lemko Wins Precedent Case over Nationalized Property," http://www.rferl.org/ content/article/1344143.html.

Index

Note: Page numbers in italics refer to illustrations.

Polish army: arrest of suspected Ukrainian nationalists, 106–7; as coercive and brutal during Ukrainian resettlement, xi, 53, 57, 60–61, 85; GO Rzeszów, 59, 85, 160n; GO Wisła, 91, 106; during Nazi invasion, 10–12; during Operation Vistula, 4, 86, 91–94, 97, 99–101, 104–5

Polish Committee of National Liberation, 26–28, 34, 37

Polish Corridor, 10; map indicating, 15

Polish United Workers' Party, 131, 133, 137–38

Polish Workers' Party, 24, 26, 90, 122

population exchange: decision to participate in, 40, 46–47; national security cited as motive for, 54, 61, 85; Operation Vistula as part of, 93; organized resistance to, 34–35, 43, 46; Poles expelled during, 126, 160n; Polish-Soviet agreement to, x, 39, 54, 57, 59–61, 84–85, 164n; Soviet refusal to accept relocated Ukrainians, 84–85; as "voluntary," 34, 53

prisoners of war, 19–20, 109, 115–16

property: legal efforts to reclaim, 141, 143–45; looting by Poles, 82; Polish expropriation of, 95; recorded in resettlement documents, 40; restrictions on return of, 138–39, 146; seized by state, 129, 131

Provisional Government of National Unity, 43, 54, 59, 85

Provisional Government of the Republic of Poland, 37

Pupczyk, Pawlo, 120, 122–23, 125

Pyrtej, Danko, 120, 122

Pyrtej, Hania. See Lozyniak, Hania (Anna) Pyrtej

Pyrtej, Liliya, 136–38

Pyrtej, Maria (Melania's mother), 10, 12; death of, 142; marriage to Seman, 16–17; Melania's wedding, 33; Operation Vistula and resettlement of,

93–97; pictured, 63; in Recovered Territories, 101, 103, 120; refusal to resettle, 46–47, 60; resettlement to Ukrainian territories, 42; separation from family, 140; in western Poland, 123–25, 127–29

Pyrtej, Melania. See Lozyniak, Melania Pyrtej

Pyrtej, Myroslava, 130, 137–38

Pyrtej, Olya Petryszak: contact with family, 130; courtship and marriage to Petro, 25, 41–43, 48–49; at Molotov Collective farm, 54–55, 57–59; and Mychajlo Fedak of OUN, 44; pictured, 69, 70, 71; resettlement to Soviet Ukraine, 43, 48–49, 52; in Soviet Ukraine, 52, 54–55, 57–59; in Stanisławów, 58–59, 136–37; visit to Lemko region, 142–43

Pyrtej, Petro (Melania's brother): and anti-Nazi resistance, 24–25; and christening of niece, 39; courtship and marriage to Olya Petryszak, 25, 41–43, 48–49; education of, 10–11, 20–22, 54; loss of property, 129; at Molotov collective farm, 54–58; pictured, 63, 64, 68, 69, 71, 78; resettlement to Soviet Ukraine, 43, 47–53, 129; reunion with family, 6–7, 137–38; separation from family, 96–97, 130; in Stanisławów, 58–59, 136–37; visit to Lemko region, 142–43, 147; and wedding of Melania, 31–33

Pyrtej, Seman (Melania's father), 100–101; death of, 142; desire to return to Smerekowiec, 139–40; loss of legal right to property, 131; marriage to Maria, 16–17; at Melania's wedding, 33–34; Operation Vistula and resettlement of, 93–97; pictured, 63; in Recovered Territories, 103–4, 120; and resettlement to Soviet Ukraine, 40, 46–47, 60; separation from family, 46–47, 133–34, 139, 142; Soviet partisans and, 26; and Stanisław Barszcz

Pyrtej, Seman (*continued*)
  (Polish military refugee), 11–12; WWI experiences, 40

quotas (kontyngenty), 18–19, 25

Recovered Territories (Ziemie Odzyskane), 98; efforts to leave and return to Lemko region, 138; government and administration in, 133; map of, *104*; Poles relocated to, 126; Ukrainians relocated to, 85–86, 90, 122, 128; use of term, 162n

Red Army. *See* Soviet Army

religion: clergy imprisoned at Jaworzno, 114–15; and exception to relocation requirements, 54, 94; Greek Catholic church in Smerekowiec pictured, *66*; Greek Catholicism, Lemkos and, 6, 16, 33, 36, 42, 50, 54, 55, 129, 133; Roman Catholicism, 54, 129; suppression of, 50, 114–15, 137; Ukrainian Orthodoxy, 42

relocation, ix, xiv, 86, 90, 95, 107–8; arrest of those resisting, 125; assimilation as objective of, 61; as "voluntary," 34. *See also* ethnic cleansing; Operation Vistula; population exchange

relocation cards issued during Operation Vistula, *74*, 138–39, 143–45

Roosevelt, Franklin D., 26, 38

Rusophilism in Lemko region, xi

Russia. *See* Soviet Union

Russkaia Bursa, 20; students at, *68*

Rusyn identity, x–xii, 3, 20, 34, 43, 50, 54, 57

Slavs, x–xi

Slovakia, 30–32

Smereczniak, Andriy, 36, 93, 127

Smereczniak, Stefania, 127–28

Smerekowiec: Greek Catholic church in, *66*; Hania's effort to recover property in, 142–47; as home of Pyrtej family,

xi, 6–7, 17, 20–21, *66*; maps indicating location of, *5*, *15*, *38*, *52*, *104*; Nazi occupation of, 9–11, 13, 18, 23–25, 27–31, 33, *65*; Nazi retreat from, 36–37; Pyrtej house, *66*; relocation of villagers, 39–40, 46–47, 60–61, 93–100; Soviet bombing and incursion in, 30–31, 37–38; Ukrainian minority permitted to return to, 132–33, 138–39; UPA partisan activity in, 81–83, 95

Śnietnica, 27–28, 31; map indicating location of, *38*

Soviet Army, 14–15, 22–31, 26–27

Soviet Ukraine: resettlement to, xi–xii, 39–40, 43, 50, 53–54; Ukrainian nationalism in, 35, 81–82, 126

Soviet Union: Curzon Line as Soviet-Polish border, 26, 38; Hitler's attack on, 22–23; influence in Polish government, 26, 131, 137; map of occupied Poland, *15*; and population exchange, 34, 39–40, 84–86; Soviet-German border agreement, x, *15*; during WWII (*see* Soviet Army)

Stalin, Joseph, 26, 38; and communism in Poland, 25–27, 37–38, 131; and conflict with Nazi Germany, 22, 26–27; death of, 134, 137; and Polish boundary negotiations, 26–27; and population exchanges, x, 34–35

Stanisławów (Ivano-Frankivsk), 7, 59, 130, 136, 142

State Repatriation Office (Państwowy Urząd Repatriacyjny, PUR), 104

Stebel's'kyi, Stepan (Khrin), 161n

Steca, Ostep, 85–86, 162n

Sudetenland, 9–10, *15*

Świerczewski, Karol, 87–90, 92–93, 130

Talerhof, 25

trains, relocation via, 4, 49–51, 92–93, 98, 100–105, 101–5, 108, 118

trenches, German conscription of labor to dig, 27–29, 31, 33